Dark Marathon

Dear Cathy,

I'm so glad we are getting to know each other. Your friendship is a blessing. May God continue to bless and guide your ministry, teaching, and home life with Mark.

Love in Christ,

Mary

6/00

Dark Marathon

The Mary Wazeter Story

The Ongoing Struggles of a World-Class Runner

Mary Wazeter
with
Gregg Lewis

Zondervan Books
Zondervan Publishing House
Grand Rapids, Michigan

Dark Marathon: The Mary Wazeter Story

Zondervan Books
are published by Zondervan Publishing House
1415 Lake Drive, S.E.
Grand Rapids, MI 49506

Library of Congress Cataloging-in-Publication Data

Wazeter, Mary.
Dark marathon : the Mary Wazeter story / by Mary Wazeter with Gregg Lewis.
ISBN 0-310-41781-3
1. Wazeter, Mary. 2. Runners—United States—Biography. 3. Scoliosis—Patients—Biography. I. Lewis, Gregg A. II. Title.
GV1061.15.W39A3 1989
616.85'26—dc19
[B] 88-35965
CIP

Printed in the United States of America

89 90 91 92 93 94 / LP / 10 9 8 7 6 5 4 3 2 1

To my Lord and Savior Jesus Christ,
The Author and Perfecter of my faith,
Source of my strength and joy;
He is all there is to life.

I would like to acknowledge
the many beloved friends and relatives
who have stood with me throughout the years,
and the countless others
who have whispered a prayer on my behalf—
especially my parents
who have so sacrificially given of their lives
in order to improve mine;
my sister, Judy, and her husband, Bill,
who have helped me to know God
in a more personal way;
my brother Gerry and his wife, Sandy,
who have loved me steadfastly and unconditionally,
and my brother David, who encouraged me
to start running, and imbued within me
a fighting spirit

Prologue

The dark drizzly February evening matched Mary's mood. After months of resisting, she was ready to surrender to hopelessness. She had exhausted all other alternatives.

"I'm taking the dog for a walk," Mary called to her mother.

"Be back before supper, dear," came the response from the kitchen. "We're having your favorite—veal parmigiana."

Mary closed the door behind her, knowing those were the last words she would ever hear her mother say.

Moments later Mary and her little dog, Rusty, a mixed-breed cross between a golden retriever and a cocker spaniel, turned from her street onto Old River Road and headed toward the pumping station on the banks of the Susquehanna River five blocks away.

Leon Wazeter spotted the familiar figure of his eighteen-year-old daughter as he drove along Old River Road on his way home from work. When he stopped, he rolled down his window and asked where she was going. Mary told him the same thing she had told her mom: she was taking the dog for a walk. He started on home. When he looked back a few moments later, Mary and Rusty had disappeared down a side street.

Mary traipsed for a while around the Wilkes-Barre, Pennsylvania, neighborhood she had lived in all her life. She had run thousands of training miles over those streets. She knew every house, every foot of pavement. She also knew where she was going and what she had to do.

Thirty minutes after closing the front door of her house, Mary scrambled up a muddy embankment to a train track that ran high over the Susquehanna on an old railroad bridge. Dragging her whimpering, terrified dog after her, Mary walked deliberately out onto the bridge, along the same rickety plank walkway she had run over so many times.

Mary couldn't see anything in the darkness below. But when she had gone almost halfway and knew she was well out over the river, she stopped. Telling herself there would be no turning back, she dropped the dog's leash, ducked under the guardrail, and stepped out onto a steel beam.

There, on a nearly invisible foot-wide perch, forty feet above the swift, icy waters, Mary ignored the whining of her dog and concentrated on maintaining her balance. Then she calmly, determinedly counted to ten and stepped off into the darkness. The winter wind muffled her scream as she plunged through the night.

Of course, Mary Wazeter's story didn't begin on that winter night of February 4, 1982. A world-class athlete doesn't suddenly decide to end it all by jumping off a bridge. Mary's decision was the outgrowth of a long, agonizing battle with emotional, physical, and spiritual turmoil, the roots of which penetrated every aspect of her being and reached back through the years to the very beginning of her athletic career.

This is her story.

Dark Marathon

Chapter 1

"Come on, Mary! We're gonna be late!" David called from the bottom of the stairs.

"Just a minute!" I yelled back as I finished lacing up my new running shoes. Moments later I joined my brother, and we left the house together to walk the six short blocks to Meyers High School.

The blazing August sun seemed unseasonably warm. But though we were dressed for the weather in shorts and T-shirts, part of my discomfort stemmed from my own excitement and uncertainty about my very first cross-country practice.

As we walked south along Old River Road, away from the river, I felt a surge of relief that David was with me. *But then I wouldn't be doing this on my own,* I told myself.

David was my only sibling still living at home. For as long as I could remember I'd looked up to him and tried to emulate him. He was a tenth-grader and a veteran member of the Meyers cross-country and track teams. I was just starting seventh grade, and this would be my first year at the combined junior and senior high school.

Even as we walked around the back side of the brick-walled football stadium and headed for the front of the school, the irony of what I was doing hit me. If anyone, at any point before that summer of 1975, had told me that my introduction to high-school life would be through sports, I would have laughed. No absurdity would have seemed less likely.

I always loved school. I enjoyed learning and gained a lot of my self-worth from doing well in my studies. But I'd grown up hating gym class. I was never among those chosen first for any team. Indeed, I could have been the inspiration for that age-old sexist description of male klutziness, "He throws like a girl." With the exception of swimming, which I loved and excelled in, sports weren't my bag.

In fifth and sixth grade I'd been a member of our elementary school's cheerleading squad. But two years of continuous practice alone in front of my bedroom mirror did nothing to improve my embarrassingly uncoordinated routine at games. I concluded that even cheerleading required more athletic ability than I'd been born with.

And yet, here I was, a month before the start of seventh grade, excitedly anticipating my first cross-country workout.

Most of the dozen runners who gathered on the front steps at the southeast corner of the school had run cross-country or track the year before. Mary was the only seventh-grader present, though others would be recruited after school started. One other girl, a senior, showed up the first day. Abby was an all-round good athlete who ran cross-country each year, primarily to get in shape for baseball. David introduced Abby to his sister before the coach came out to welcome everyone and give instructions.

When Coach Watkins appeared, he was wearing jean shorts, sandals, and a T-shirt. In his late twenties, with brown hair and a mustache, his build denied that he was a runner. And he wasn't. But he knew plenty about it. Through reading and research he'd become a very effective and experienced cross-country coach.

"The first thing you're going to do is run together over to Kirby Park on the other side of the river," Coach Watkins explained as he quickly surveyed the group of us seated on the steps in front of him. "I know this is the first day, so if some of you have to stop and walk, don't worry. Those of you who don't know the course, stick with the runners who ran on last year's team."

To me, the youngest person present, the coach gave an added word of instruction. "Don't worry if you can't make it all the way. Abby will run with you."

As the team took off and Abby trotted alongside me, I confessed my own misgivings to her.

"If you need to stop and walk, Mary, I'll walk with you," she said. "I won't leave you."

Determined not to hold anyone back, I tried to keep David and the other lead runners in sight as we ran back up along Old River Road, through my own neighborhood. I still felt strong as we passed my street and turned off the main thoroughfare to cut through the side streets toward the river. I was beginning to think I might make it all the way when we reached the railroad embankment. The first feelings of uncertainty didn't hit me until I climbed up on the tracks and saw the runners ahead of me pounding the narrow plank walkway spanning the bridge.

Though I'd lived within six blocks of that bridge all my life, I'd never been out on it. It had always been off-limits for me and the other kids in the community. A boardwalk high above a deep river and less than three feet away from passing freight trains was no place to play. Also, the bridge was a popular hangout where local motorcycle riders and a tough crowd of older teenagers gathered to drink and, rumor had it, do drugs.

Noticing, or perhaps only guessing my hesitancy, Abby recruited one of the other runners to cross the bridge in front of me. "I'll run right behind you," she encouraged. "Just keep your eyes on the walk ahead of you and don't look down."

The thud, thud, thud of running shoes on wood echoed eerily up and around the black steel superstructure that arched into the sky overhead. Even without looking down, I could sense the emptiness beneath me and, between the footfalls, I could hear the steady rushing of water flowing far below.

But I kept running. We finally reached the opposite bank and then headed upstream along the top of the levee until we came to the grassy expanse of Kirby Park.

"Hey, look!" one of the runners announced to the group. "Mary made it!" As I basked in the congratulations of my teammates and the surprised approval of Coach Watkins, I thought back to the important day, just a few months before, when I'd discovered running.

It had happened in gym class, of all places. Everyone in sixth grade was required to perform six different events as part of the nationally standardized Presidential Fitness Test. I'd taken the test in fourth and fifth grades, but I'd never won the certificate awarded to those whose total scores exceed the predetermined level of performance established for that age. Knowing my third try would be my last, I wanted one of those certificates.

As expected, I did abominably in the softball throw and only average in such events as the standing broad jump and the 40-yard dash. Though I did better than some of the other girls, my mediocre performances seemed particularly inadequate because my best friend, Lisa DelBalso, was terrific at everything. So, by comparison, the test looked like one more unpleasant failure for me. Until the last event—the 600-yard run.

Unlike the kids who practically staggered to the finish line, I finished my run feeling strong. And when the phys ed teacher announced the times, I'd clocked the fastest time for the 600 of all the girls in the school and bested a number of boys. My performance won me the certificate I'd wanted. And just as important to me, I'd beaten Lisa.

The top-scoring students in each event were invited to compete against the best from the other schools around the city. After that competition I took home a fourth-place ribbon for the 600-yard run and a changing attitude toward athletics. Feeling encouraged for the first time in my life about a physical competition, I allowed myself to think, *Maybe this doesn't have to end here. It could be a new beginning.*

I had never been a fast runner. But I began to think maybe my talent lay in stamina and determination. David encouraged me to run with him and some of his cross-country buddies. I surprised them and myself by keeping up with these older guys, both in the pace they set in their workouts and in the distances run. My legs got perceptibly stronger and my technique improved as David coached me throughout the summer. So by the time August 1 rolled around, I didn't need much persuasion to show up for the first practice.

Still, I couldn't get over the fact that I enjoyed running. The more I ran, the better it felt—almost as natural as walking. The satisfying sense of exertion and fatigue seemed to heighten all my senses and sweeten even the most ordinary of daily routines. Hot showers had never felt so soothing. Food had never tasted so good.

The second day of practice Mary did two miles. And by the end of the first week she could run four without a break. Within a couple weeks she consistently outran Abby and held her own with some of the boys. Her coach and teammates were impressed. And their growing respect gave her a small measure of confidence with which to face the opening of school—an event she anticipated with a mixture of excitement and trepidation.

As high schools go Meyers' 1800 students didn't make for an exceptionally large school. But for a twelve-year-old kid, fresh out of elementary school, the crowded hallways looked as ominous as New York City at rush hour.

I figured I had one big advantage over many other first-year students: my brother David was a popular kid and knew a lot of teachers and students. I needed that advantage because I didn't know very many of my seventh-grade classmates. I had gone from first to sixth grade at Mackin Elementary School across the city as part of a gifted-student program. My classmates for six years had been drawn from around the city and now attended various high schools throughout the community. So the only friendly faces I recognized were those of a couple kids from my neighborhood and my church and a handful of girls I knew from Girl Scouts. Outside this fairly small clique, I felt like a foreigner.

It didn't help my uneasiness that I felt unattractive, with my wire-rim glasses and my gangly little-girl physique. Just walking through those hallways alongside hundreds of older, more physically mature girls made me feel conspicuously out of place.

But what seemed even more foreboding than the immense sea of strangers was the building itself. Including the football stadium attached at the back, this imposing, three-story blond brick building covered nearly an entire city block. My greatest fear was not meeting new classmates and teachers, or even adjusting to a tougher class schedule. What I dreaded most of all was the horrible and embarrassing possibility of getting separated from my small group of friends and becoming lost in the sprawling labyrinth of hallways and stairwells that honeycombed the massive building.

On the third day of classes, my worst nightmare came true. When I finished lunch I looked around and realized all my friends had finished and gone. With no one to walk with to my next class, I was on my own. I remembered only that my Math class was on the second floor. But when I found what I thought looked like a familiar hallway, I had no idea which classroom was mine. Slowly, uncertainly, I walked down the hall and then back, glancing in each door I passed, hoping to see a set of faces I could associate with the previous two days of Math. I'd left my schedule with the room numbers at home on my dresser, so the numerals on the doors were useless.

The halls were nearly empty now; classes had started. I turned and walked down the hall and back again. And again.

On what must have been the fifth or sixth pass, I saw my teacher. I stepped into the room, hoping to slip unnoticed to my seat. But the moment I walked through the doorway, the entire class of students erupted into laughter. They'd been watching me wander back and forth for five minutes. But what they found funny left me mortified with shame.

That same week we elected student council representatives for seventh grade. I volunteered. But when the vote came, another girl had beaten me in what seemed like a very personal rejection by my peers.

All in all, my first week of high school wasn't one of my favorite experiences. I survived the daily pressure by looking forward to the escape of cross-country practice after school. And though the regular routine gradually became easier as I made new acquaintances and proved myself to teachers, my first week at Meyers set the pattern for the year. The one place I could really relax and feel totally accepted was at the end of the school day, running with the cross-country team.

I relished the easy camaraderie of the guys, their teasing and gradual acceptance. David's friends called him "Waz," so my nickname became "Little Waz." I think I surprised them, the coach, and even David with my competitive drive.

By the time a number of teams from around the valley convened for the first invitational meet of the season at Kirby Park, I already knew I was the second-best female runner on the Meyers team. The team's leader, Sharon Jarrell, a junior, had been away in August when we had begun training. But in the short time since Sharon had joined the team, she had become my first running hero. She was a tough, experienced runner from whom I could learn a lot. And I was anxious to see how I would fare against her and the best girls from other high schools.

As the youngest girl in the race, I didn't feel much pressure. I knew the course because we practiced on it every day. David had warned me not to start too fast and burn myself out. So when the gun sounded, I settled into a steady pace some distance behind Sharon and the other leaders. As the race developed, a number of runners dropped off the pace and I passed one after another. On the last straightaway stretch of the 1.7-mile course I had enough kick to pass one more girl and finish in third place.

Sharon took first. But for years, the scene I would remember most vividly would be the sight of the second-place runner who finished just a few yards ahead of me. The girl, a senior from another school, had run so hard she passed out and crumpled to the ground just after crossing the finish line.

My teammates and all the guys from the boys' team swarmed around to congratulate me. David was ecstatic. "You don't even look tired! You look like you could do it all over again!"

I couldn't have felt any happier than I did that afternoon in winning my first trophy and making a big impression, not only on my teammates but on the coaches and runners of every other school around. Yet even as I soaked in the warm praise and accepted the pats on the back, I couldn't get the image of that second-place finisher out of my mind. In contrast to her exhaustion I didn't even feel very tired.

Her example was enough to convince me that cross-country competition needed to be an all-or-nothing proposition. And I determined to do whatever it took to succeed.

Chapter 2

Since there was no official cross-country competition for junior-high girls and I wasn't yet eligible for the varsity team, I ran in meets with the junior-high boys. This forced me to stretch myself. I usually did well enough to finish somewhere in the middle of the pack, beating about as many boys as beat me. But the recognition and affirmation I earned through the fall established a reputation that carried me through the winter until track season began in the spring.

Then one unseasonably warm, sunny April day, I sat down to eat Sunday dinner with my family. Dad sat at his usual place at the head of the table. Mom was still bustling around in the kitchen while David and I waited patiently for the usually sumptuous Sunday fare.

As a seventh-grade girl on the front edge of adolescence, I seldom stopped to appreciate my family, let alone ponder and analyze the mix of personalities that made us unique. Yet I dearly loved my folks and my three older siblings.

Leon Wazeter, a district sales manager for World Book, was in his mid-fifties. His affable, people-loving personality and the strong work ethic instilled by his Polish-Catholic heritage probably explained his success as a salesman. Edith Wazeter had a quieter, more soft-spoken nature packed into a petite energetic body. Like Mary's dad, she had grown up in the Wilkes-Barre community where the family still lived. Her ethnic background was Welsh Presbyterian. Since neither of Mary's parents felt willing to give up their childhood faiths, Mary and the other Wazeter children grew up in a rather ecumenical family. So for Mary, a belief in God and strong convictions of right and wrong were part of her heritage.

With their Polish and Welsh ancestry, the family's roots ran deep into the mining history of the northeastern Pennsylvania mountains. But, as befitting the children of an encyclopedia salesman, the Wazeter kids were all taught early to value education and books. Gerry, Mary's oldest brother, had already graduated from King's College in political science and government. Judy, who was nine years older than Mary, was about to finish her undergraduate work in special education at Bloomsburg State College. Then there was tenth-grader David and, finally, Mary, who'd been born when both her parents were in their forties. Like many youngest children, Mary had a lot of footsteps to follow and a lot of big shoes to fill.

As a whole, our family was achievement-oriented. My parents tried to provide us with all the opportunities they could afford. They paid for music lessons and never missed a concert or a recital. Dad was at every one of my races and David's—often volunteering to help drive the team to away meets. Mom made it to any meet that didn't conflict with her office schedule. They couldn't have been more encouraging and supportive.

While my folks always expected us to do our best at whatever we attempted, I can't say I felt like they constantly pushed me. I did a good enough job of pushing myself. And I always had the challenging models of three older siblings to egg me on.

One example of Judy's influence on me and on my values occurred during the year I was in the fifth grade. She was already in college when she wrote me a fairly typical big-sis-to-little-sis letter. But in addition to bits and pieces about college life, Judy included a lot of sisterly advice:

> How's school? I hope you're doing your homework more by yourself than you did last year. . . . Are you going to take ballet? I think you should try to find some type of sewing or knitting class. A lot of girls down here have afghans and shawls and all sorts of things that they make in their spare time. I wish I had started something like that at *your* age. . . . Anyway, don't waste your time watching TV. . . . When I was your age, I did too. Believe me, you'll be SORRY. I wish I hadn't wasted so much time.

While I never could get the hang of knitting (my left-handedness complicated the learning process), I did heed Judy's warning about television. I pretty much quit watching the tube in fifth grade, and when I did watch, I'd remember Judy's letter and feel guilty.

So that Sunday dinner in April of my seventh grade stands out in my memory. No sooner had Mom put the roast on the table and Dad said a brief grace than David looked at me from across the table.

"Aren't you going to race in the Cherry Blossom Run this afternoon?"

He was referring to the big Wilkes-Barre annual 5-mile roadrace scheduled for a little later in the day.

I reached for the potatoes and gave him an off-hand reply. "I hadn't thought much about it." That was at least partly true. I had not seriously considered running for a couple reasons: the distance of the race and the fact that I didn't know any girls who ran roadraces.

"Why not?" he prodded.

"I don't want to run by myself." I shrugged.

"Well, it's not too late to change your mind."

He kept talking, and as soon as I realized he was serious, I left the table to change. David and my folks had to hurry through dinner just to get me to the starting line in time.

I had no idea how to run a 5-mile race. So I took off cautiously and slowly picked up the pace. The herd of runners at the start quickly thinned out as we wound our way through

Wilkes-Barre. Having never run a roadrace before, I found the variety of streets and buildings and scenery interesting and enjoyable. As the race progressed, my strength held up. The people standing and sitting along the way cheered and shouted encouragement as I passed, giving the race an entirely different feel from the usually lonely sport of cross-country running. I got an extra boost as the course wound along Riverside Drive and Pickering Street, and I raced through my own neighborhood to the cheers of relatives and friends.

That day I finished the Cherry Blossom Run as the first and only female finisher. The next day the local newspaper printed a picture of all the winners, referring to me as "the lone girl finisher." But even more significant than the publicity and the trophy I took home was the experience itself. I had discovered the joy of roadracing.

Track season passed and my times kept improving. But already I was looking forward to another big local roadrace—the Back Mountain Bicentennial Run—to be held a few miles from Wilkes-Barre in July. Ten miles promised to be the longest I had ever run, so I went out to the course a week ahead of time and ran it with a friend just to make sure I could make it. My cross-country teammate, Sharon, planned to run too, so I didn't want to be embarrassed.

The day of the race dawned rainy and cool. I started back in the pack at a conservative pace. For ten long miles I trudged through the rain, up and down mountains. But again, as I had in the Cherry Blossom, I enjoyed the variety of scenery—this time it was lakes and fields and beautiful mountain homes. And I crossed the finish line after the distance with something left.

Sharon won the women's division of the race, but I won a trophy for youngest finisher. And once more my picture appeared in the paper with the winners. It seemed the longer the distance, the better suited a race was for me. I'd never been blessed with natural speed, but I was beginning to realize I'd been gifted with stamina. The hard, uphill climbs became a challenge, a welcome change of pace from the long flat straights. The concentration and discipline required to make it to the finish line gave me an inexpressible satisfaction. And I found myself actually enjoying running past the point of exhaustion, gutting it out at the end of a grueling race. After just two experiences, roadracing was in my blood.

Cross-country season the fall of eighth grade provided more and better competition for Mary. She still wasn't old enough to qualify for varsity, so she had to compete again with the junior-high boys. But she trained with Sharon and they pushed each other hard in practice. Sharon finished her senior season with a fourth place in the state-championship cross-country meet for high-school girls.

A few weeks after cross-country season ended, Chuck Thoma, who helped coach Meyers' cross-country team and often ran with Mary, talked her into running yet another roadrace. This one was the annual Berwick Run for the Diamonds, one of the oldest in the country and the premier roadrace in northeastern Pennsylvania.

The rules for this race required all official entrants to be at least seventeen years old. But there was nothing to prevent me from running unofficially, just for the fun of it. So on Thanksgiving day I took my place at the starting line in front of the town's YMCA with 400 other runners, including Sharon.

Chuck, a close family friend in his early twenties who was like a big brother to me, had volunteered to run the race at my side to coach and pace me. So when the gun sounded, we started in my usual style—slow and steady. As the runners began to spread out, we gradually picked up speed. Chuck kept our time on his watch, and it was encouraging to hear his reports that we were improving our time with each mile that clipped by.

The forty-degree weather seemed perfect for running—cool enough to prevent overheating, but not so cold as to make breathing difficult. As we approached the end of the 9-mile course, Chuck and I were both surprised at my freshness.

The last mile of the Berwick race always takes place down a long boulevard right through the heart of town. Crowds of people lined both sides of the roadway to cheer the runners to the finish. A couple times I cringed to hear spectators exclaim in surprise, "Look at that little boy!" I knew they were talking about me because I'd cut my hair short at the beginning of eighth grade. I wanted to stop and shout, "Hey, I'm a girl!" But I just kept running, a little faster.

As Chuck and I ran down that boulevard, an incredible thing happened. A wave of applause and cheers rolled with us for the entire mile, building and cresting until it reached a roaring crescendo at the finish line. In my brief running career, I had never experienced another thrill like it.

I knew from Chuck's watch I had run a good race. And after accepting his congratulations, we walked around near the finish line to cool down and wait for the other finishers. Over three minutes later we spotted Sharon coming down the boulevard.

"Here comes the first woman!" shouted someone in the crowd. And as Sharon crossed the finish line to a deafening ovation, I wanted to scream, "What about me?" Of course I knew I couldn't expect a prize as an unofficial entrant, but my brief victory was overshadowed by the bitterness of regret, and my thoughts tumbled about in turmoil. *At least I should have gotten some extra recognition and applause.* I felt like cursing my haircut and my boyish build.

Once all the racers had crossed the line, Chuck and I (along with my personal cheering section—Dad, Judy, and David) slipped into the nearby gymnasium to witness the awards ceremony. The race organizers gave Sharon a nice trophy and the crowd gave her another big hand. And while I was happy for my friend, I couldn't help thinking, *It should have been me.*

At the close of the ceremony, after all the pictures had been taken and the reporters had made their notes, Chuck and I went up to congratulate Sharon. The moment she spotted us, she held out the trophy. "I can't accept this. I want you to have it."

But I didn't feel right about taking it. After all, Sharon had been the first official female finisher. I shook my head.

Sharon pressed the trophy into my hands insistently. "Take it, Mary. You won it."

So I went home with a trophy and the reassuring feeling that Sharon Jarrell was not only a great model as a runner, but a considerate friend. She had been my running idol and example for over a year; now, for the first time, I'd beaten her in a race.

Our friendship and competitive rivalry continued. The next spring when we both ran in the Cherry Blossom Run, Sharon took first place for women. And in the summer we both entered the Back Mountain race; I took home the first-place trophy and the award for youngest finisher.

Despite my success and fast-growing love for running during seventh and eighth grades, I tried hard to avoid the stereotype of an athlete. In seventh grade I performed as one of the Von Trapp children in a school production of "The Sound of Music." In eighth grade I played in "Music Man." I kept up my piano lessons, played a solo in the annual spring chorale program in eighth grade, and maintained an A average in class, working hard to project a well-rounded image.

Yet my life turned around 180 degrees during my junior-high years. Throughout elementary school I had abhorred team sports and depended, instead, on my top grades for peer approval. Now, though my grades were as good as ever, I still didn't feel comfortable in school. When I ran for student council and lost again in eighth grade, it confirmed in my mind an undeniable lack of popularity.

Tied up with my concern about being stereotyped and being unpopular was a continuing dissatisfaction with my looks. To avoid an embarrassing recurrence of the Berwick race, I let my hair grow long, and carried a comb in my hand or stuck in my hair whenever I ran, in practice or in races. The guys on the team teased me about the comb, but I didn't mind. I saw it all as part of the image I wanted to project—tough but feminine.

I didn't feel confident about the "feminine" part, though. I continued to feel shy and unattractive with any guys other than my running friends. And I never felt like I quite measured up to several of my girl friends who seemed to be among the prettiest and most popular in school.

But the "tough" runner image no one would deny. Even before Mary reached ninth grade and qualified for high-school competition, she had made a name for herself in her part of the state as an up-and-coming runner. And it was as a runner that she was best known at school and in the community.

Her yearbooks from seventh and eighth grades, filled with messages from friends, classmates, and teachers, paint a pretty clear picture of Mary's image:

> *Mary, now that you're a superstar, you're going to have to keep training. . . . You're a great girl and a good friend.*
>
> *Mary, To the best runner in the whole school. I hope you win more trophies than your house can hold.*
>
> *Mary, to a great friend and track star. Now that Sharon is going, we're going to hear your name for state champion.*
>
> *Next year is your big year. District champ. I know you can't wait to start running again.*
>
> *Mary Baby, One of those crazy cross-country runners. I don't know why we do it, but God knows we'll never stop. Thanks so much for running with me and putting up with my complaining about races, training, etc. We've had a lot of fantastic times together. And I just want you to know that I respect you and admire you as an athlete and as a person. I'm gonna keep in touch and have Chuckie let me know if you're dogging it. Gee, Mary, I'm really gonna miss you. Thanks for being my friend. All my love, Sharon.*
>
> *Good luck in everything, including the Olympics.*

As I read over those quotes and a lot of others in my yearbooks the summer before ninth grade, I realized that it was running that had brought me the satisfaction of acclaim. And if I believed those glowing yearbook entries—and I wanted to—it was running that offered the greatest promise of success.

Running had provided my identity. And I thanked God for the special ability he'd given me.

I was Mary Wazeter, promising young runner. Now I had only to fulfill the promise.

Chapter 3

Bob entered my life the summer between eighth and ninth grades. He'd been the star of the boys' championship junior-high cross-country team the previous season. He had talked to me and teased me in practice, and a couple times during the year he'd seen me at a school dance and asked me to dance with him. Of all the guys on the team, he was the one I thought could be special. Bob was good-looking, about 5′9″, with wavy brown hair and big brown eyes. He made nearly straight A's, played in the band, and had loads of friends.

I figured I was just fooling myself to imagine he had any interest in me though. Since he was a year ahead of me in school, we never had any classes together and seldom saw each other anywhere but at running practice.

But I ran into Bob a lot more that summer—especially at Miner Park, a favorite gathering place where a lot of my friends went to play games and meet for trips to nearby pizza or ice-cream spots. We talked quite a bit, and I heard through the grapevine that he liked me. But I still didn't know what to expect one sweltering evening when he rode up beside me on his bike as I was leaving the park.

"Mind if I walk you home?" he asked.

My heart gave a crazy kind of lurch. "No," I managed to reply with a smile.

Actually, he didn't exactly "walk" me home. The more accurate word would be "escorted." He rode his bike, backpedaling and braking to stay beside me as I walked. We made rather transparent small talk, and I wondered if he had more on his mind than the weather.

He did. And when he finally asked me to go steady with him, my heart kicked into a trip-hammer beat, like the adrenaline surge just before a tough track meet.

We spent a lot of time together the rest of that summer. But since neither of us drove, our social life was somewhat limited. We played a lot of tennis and ran together. I'd go to his house for cookouts with his family, or he'd come to my house for dinner with mine. We would sit on the front porch and talk for hours. And the more time we spent together, the more wonderful love seemed.

By the time school started, I had never felt happier. For the first time in my life I had a real boyfriend; like my most popular friends, I had a social life to talk about. And dating a popular older boy like Bob made me feel more a part of Meyers High School than I had the previous two years.

Running promised to be better than ever too. And not just because I could see Bob at practice.

For two years I had been too young to run for the varsity girls' team and had always run under the shadow of Sharon Jarrell. So ninth-grade cross-country season was going to be my first time in the sun. Though only a freshman, I quickly established myself as the number-one runner on the girls' team. Consistently I won meets all through the season. But it was the district and state competition that I was training for. Everything else was just a season-long warm-up.

Running became not only a priority for me, it became a commitment from my entire family. As usual, Dad cheered for me at every meet. Mom took off work as often as possible and scheduled family dinners late—after cross-country practice. And

Dad helped organize a booster club for Meyers' running teams. Finally the commitment paid off.

Four hundred runners from thirty schools took part in Pennsylvania's Interscholastic Athletic Association District 2 Cross-Country Championship. Mary captured first place among girls from Class AA schools, and was satisfied to finish second overall to Cheryl Wallace, a runner for rival Valley West High School, who won first among Class AAA competitors. They both broke the old district championship time set by Sharon Jarrell the year before.

So in her first year of varsity competition Mary won a district championship. The local paper carried a story, and students and teachers alike called out congratulations the next Monday morning as she walked down the halls of the school. Mary was already anticipating her first state championship meet the following Saturday.

On the morning of November 5, the day of the state race, I awakened feeling wretched. Though I had told myself all week I was just glad to be running at state and couldn't really expect to win any medal as a freshman runner, I was so uptight I hadn't been able to sleep. Several times in the night I'd had to hurry to the bathroom because of my nausea. And now I tried in vain to control my emotions by giving myself a lecture: *Settle down, Mary, or you won't be able to run worth anything.*

A few hours later, as I lined up with almost two hundred other runners at the starting line on the Penn State golf course in State College, Pennsylvania, the nausea intensified. No sooner did the gun sound and the lead runners sprint out than my body finally succumbed to my nerves—and I threw up. For almost a mile after my stomach had emptied itself, my insides convulsed again and again with the dry heaves. By the time I calmed the physiological storm inside, the race was half over. And by then, my discouragement combined with my weakened physical condition made it impossible to gain on the leaders. In fact, runner after runner passed me. I finished forty-eighth.

Although I crossed the finish line feeling physically better than I had felt at the outset, I couldn't hold back the tears of disappointment. My teammates tried to cheer me up. "Look how many people you beat, Mary." But their words were like salt on my wounded spirit. I felt so depressed I didn't even hang around for the awards ceremony—I didn't think I could stand to look at the girls who had beaten me in the biggest race of my life.

I wasn't expecting to win, but based on my previous times, I had expected to finish at least in the top thirty. And my dream had been to win an All-State medal by finishing in the top twenty. Never in my worst nightmares would I have expected to come in as low as forty-eighth.

I went home not just defeated, but embarrassed. On Monday morning, just a week after my triumphant return to school as the heralded district champion, I felt like hiding in my locker. I imagined all my teachers and classmates watching me and thinking, "Mary may be good around here, but she just can't compete with the best runners in the state."

Sometimes I had those same thoughts about myself. But I kept thinking *I'm better than forty-eighth. I know I am.* And I determined to prove it to everyone when track season rolled around in the spring.

Despite my disappointment, ninth grade continued to be my best year yet in school. I got more involved in school activities: chorus, key club, speech, and debate. And I still had Bob.

With an eye toward track season, Mary trained all winter for the first time in three years of running. Bob ran with her a lot of days. So when spring arrived, she was ready. She won the women's division of the Cherry Blossom Run. And she came out a triple winner in most of the track meets the Meyers team entered—regularly winning the 2-mile, the mile, and the 880 events. Plus, she ran an 880 anchor leg on the squad's 2-mile relay team, which took a number of firsts.

I won the Class AA District championship in the 2-mile and

the mile, earning my second trip to a state championship. I feared getting sick again, but I kept my nerves under control and came in fifth in the 2-mile, qualifying me for my first all-state medal. I had vindicated myself after my disappointing cross-country season. Yet, whenever I reviewed my performance in the state championship 2-mile race, I remembered how I had run in second place most of the race until three girls blew past me on the final lap. *If I had only had some kick left at the end,* I told myself, *I could easily have held on for second.*

I vowed to do better the next year. The more I thought about it, the more I believed that if I worked hard enough, I just might be state champion some day.

But the increased commitment to running during the summer between ninth and tenth grades seemed to separate me from my friends. The group of girls I ran around with were dating and going to parties. Some of my friends seemed to have attracted the interest of more than one boy, while I still had only Bob. As much as I cared about him, I began to wonder if anyone else would ever want to go out with me.

As the summer wore on, my friends didn't call me anymore—I had to call them. Bobby left town on vacation, and on July 25 I wrote in my diary: "Loneliness is moving in on me again. I miss Bobby a lot. . . . Thank God Judy is home. At least she's somebody to talk to."

My emotional state probably had a lot to do with my poor showing in a 3-mile race at Pocono Downs Race Track the next day. My diary entry for July 26 gives the details: "Race was a disaster today. Got beat by Cheryl Wallace and Elaine Yurek. Cheryl went out fast and I just let her go. But that won't ever happen again, I promise. I was so depressed after the race. I went out with a couple friends afterward to cheer up, but I didn't have too good a time. Just can't help it. I feel out of place. Don't know many kids from other schools. My friends know all of them. But I doubt anyone even looked at me."

My feelings of social failure even affected my training. One night I wrote in my diary: "I didn't run today. I just wasn't up to going on my own. I don't deserve to be good with that kind of attitude. But I'm not going to worry about it."

By the thirtieth of August I screwed up my determination again and wrote: "If I want to be good at running, I'm going to have to forget about other things. Not just talk about running, but do it. It has to come first. I have to make the choice if I want to do that. Everyone at school associates me with running anyway. That's what I should concentrate on."

That night I made my decision to drop piano lessons, hoping this change in my routine would give me more time to train. I vowed to start my sophomore year at school with the singlemindedness I knew was needed to be a winner. I told myself, *If I can't be popular, at least I'll be successful.*

The cross-country season began on a good note. I ran better times than ever in some of the early meets. But what I set my heart on having was another district championship and a better-than-ever showing at the state meet.

Those were the goals I envisioned just ahead of me with every workout, every mile I ran. In fact, every race, every practice run, I imagined I was in the state championship race, pushing hard for the finish.

One Friday night in September, I sat at home doing homework and writing Judy until I knew the Meyers football game would be past half-time. Then I walked the six blocks to the stadium and went in to find my friends, so I could go with them to Burger King after the game.

As I entered the football stadium the scoreboard lights signaled that the game was still in the third quarter. After walking nearly the entire length of the stands, searching for somebody to sit with for the remainder of the game, I was reminded of my reason for not coming earlier. All of my closest friends were either cheerleaders or majorettes. And Bobby had to sit with the other members of the school band. So there was no one else I knew very well to chum with.

It seemed that most of the girls in the stands were spending more time talking with the guys or seeing who was sitting with whom than they spent watching the game. That only made me feel more abnormal because I was too shy to flirt. And I still didn't think any boy besides Bobby would be interested in me.

Late that night, right after returning from the local Burger King where I had managed to relax and have a good time with my friends, I wrote my reactions to the evening in my diary, concluding: "Next time I'm going to wait until I know the game is almost over."

But it wasn't just the awkwardness I felt at football games that convinced me of my social ineptitude. Despite my continuing success in cross-country, self-doubts hounded me. Three diary entries show my struggle:

> September 30: Today we voted for homecoming queen. I'm always thinking of homecoming, student council elections, etc. I can't get them out of my mind. I'm forever saying to myself, "Act poised, pretty, like a homecoming queen." Wish I could just forget about that. I know it's not really important.

> October 9: I finally have my hair exactly the way I want it. Hope the permanent lasts more than a month. Now I look the way I want, but my personality needs help. . . . I will not put myself down. But no talking about running and no thinking about state.

On October 10 my history teacher complained to my cross-country coach that I hadn't been paying attention in class. Evidently his assessment was that I had been letting my running success go to my head. The coach called me in and related the history teacher's complaint.

> The way I feel today is disgusted with myself. I don't know why, I just am. Maybe it sounds like self-pity, but how come I'm always the one getting criticized? I think I'm a misfit. Still feel I have an inferiority complex which I've tried so hard to get rid of. Next minute they say I'm conceited. Deep down I don't think I'm great at

all. Either I'm putting myself down, which is wrong, or my tone of voice makes people think I'm conceited. I guess the best thing to do is be myself. But that's hard because my true self is mean on the surface. I'm too quick to voice my criticism of others. There just aren't many people I'm at ease with anymore. I'm always wondering if I'm acting right. I've tried so hard to be liked. Tomorrow I won't say one bad thing about anybody, even if it kills me.

Chapter 4

When Bob decided we ought to start dating other people, I was shocked and hurt. "It'll be better for you because you'll get the chance to date a lot of other guys," he tried to explain. "And it'll be better for both of us because we'll get a chance to test our relationship."

Despite those assurances, I was crushed. *Maybe I'm just not good enough for him,* I thought. Suddenly there was a big hole in my life, and the only way I knew to fill it was to try to do something to prove myself once and for all.

On October 25 I told my diary:

> Can't believe district is tomorrow. Time really does go fast. I'm not nervous this time. I worked too hard to be nervous. I actually believe I can win and I'm going to keep believing it until I'm done tomorrow. I'd love to run until I'm totally exhausted. I always recover too soon after a race.

The next day I won my second Class AA district cross-country championship. But for the second year in a row I finished second in the overall race to the AAA champion, senior Cheryl Wallace. And that night I poured out my frustration in writing:

> Well, the dream is over. I didn't win. . . . Not winning didn't really matter. It was coming in twenty seconds behind Cheryl that really hurt. All that about, "Oh, I'm going to give her a race." It just went down the drain.

> I thought running was the only thing that mattered. But it's not. The most important thing is being happy. And I'm good enough to make myself happy. No sense being bitter. It only makes you frustrated and you end up not running well anyway.

For the next week I battled my emotions in an attempt to try to keep my spirits up for state meet. On November 2 I wrote in my diary:

> Tomorrow I'm off for state. I can't really believe it. Seems like it's all I've thought about since track season. Hundreds of times I've envisioned myself leading, coming through that finish line first. Then I think about how happy I'd be. I'd finally feel proud and confident. Not that I should feel I'm nothing now. But I want to prove to myself that something can be done if I set my mind to it. I want to totally rid myself of this inferiority complex. I wouldn't feel cocky if I won, but I think I'd feel I could finally be my own person and happy to be who I am. If I pray, pray, pray, relax and stay confident, I'm sure I'll do well. I won't give up and no one is going to talk me out of anything. I won't put myself down. And remember, "Enthusiasm makes the difference."

But enthusiasm wasn't enough. Neither was my determination to try once more to run to the point of exhaustion. I finished nineteenth, the next-to-the last person to qualify for an All-State medal.

I did hang around after my own race to root for Cheryl in the AAA championship. And she gave all her friends something to cheer about. She and another girl were battling for third as they approached the finish. The other runner tried to give an extra kick and pulled slightly ahead. But in the last few yards of the race, Cheryl caught her again and literally threw herself across the finish in third place and crumpled to the ground. The crowd cheered her effort, but suddenly fell silent when she failed to move. Two medics rushed over, turned her on her back, and revived her with smelling salts. And as slower runners crossed the finish line, Cheryl was carried away.

I worried about Cheryl until word came a short while later saying she had been sick with the flu before the race and that she was all right now. But even greater than my concern was my admiration. I thought, *If I could just once run to the limits of my physical abilities like that, no telling how good I could be. I'm always too strong at the end of a race; I have to quit holding back.*

November 5, the day after the state meet, I reflected more about my state championship:

> Disappointed and crushed is how I feel. I ended up in nineteenth place; I never dreamed it would be so bad. Cheryl got third. What I learned was not to set my goals so high and unrealistically. I think if I'd placed in the top ten, that would have been great. But the rest of the season tenth seemed terrible. I had no idea I'd have to work that hard to get nineteenth! Next year I'm going to aim for the top ten and that's all. I'm also going to stop dreaming and think realistically. It doesn't help to think races over and over in your head; it's better to just go and run till you're dead. Forget the place and whom you're running against, just go after who's in front and stay with them.

In addition to my running disappointments, my social life didn't live up to Bob's predictions. Guys weren't beating down the door to take me out; in fact, no one asked me out.

But not all my activities were destined to end in failure. I had tried out earlier that fall and won one of the lead parts in a drama production of Edward Albee's "The Sand Box." When we put on the play for a school assembly, it was a big hit. My character, an old grandmother, was especially well received. That night we performed in district play competition, after which I wrote in my diary:

> I had a great time on stage today. I love it so much. But I told myself because we were so good at assembly doesn't mean we'd win tonight. But we did. It's such a good feeling to win. No runner-up. But really win. No one person won for us. But since I did have a lead part, I know I had to be good or we wouldn't have won. I know it's nothing to get cocky about. But it's enough to show that I'm a winner. Not always. But it isn't impossible.

When I went back to school the next Monday, I got more congratulations for the play than I ever had for running. It felt good to know I could make a big splash in something besides sports. And I began to feel better about myself. I went to a dance that next week and for the first time in months was asked to dance by two guys.

But the good feelings never seemed to last that fall. The day before Thanksgiving and another Berwick Marathon, I wrote:

> I wish I could do good, but I don't deserve it because I've been such a dogger. Tomorrow I swear I'll run till I'm dead!

The next evening, November 23, I wrote:

> Today was another great day. I got second. Never dreamed I'd do that well. It helps to set reasonable goals. If I'd said I wanted first, I would have been disappointed.

The local paper carried a picture of me with my second-place trophy along with an article headlined: "State Crown Goal of Meyers's Runner." The article began:

> Little Mary Wazeter of Meyers would love to run her way to a state title some day. And with three years to accomplish the feat, the 15-year-old Wilkes-Barre runner is off to a good start. . . .
>
> "I love to run," said the petite runner. "I run some eight miles several times a week. It's exhilarating.". . .
>
> "I would love to be a state champion," offered the Meyers sophomore. "However, that might be unrealistic."

I'd learned my lesson. No more big dreams. My fantasy bubbles always burst.

Still, my limited success at Berwick and winning the district and then the regional play competition weren't inoculation against my doubts. Just before Christmas I wrote:

> I thank God tomorrow is the last day of school. I'm so mixed up. I don't know what I want or how I feel about anything. I guess the main thing is I don't feel secure about myself. I'm always thinking to myself, "Am I acting the right way? Am I too serious? Too silly? Do I appear to be at ease?"

Contrasting the experience of one of my best friends with mine only made me feel more inadequate than ever. Boys called her constantly. And when we went to a dance, she always got twice as many offers to dance as I did.

It helped when Bob called just before Christmas to ask if we could start dating again. I quickly agreed, and my excitement to have Bob back was only slightly tempered by his suggestion that we promise to be honest if either one of us saw someone else we'd like to date.

On New Year's Day I made my last entry of the year in my old diary by summarizing my feelings about myself and setting some new goals:

> I feel so mean. All I ever think about is myself. It's about time I started thinking of others. This next year I'm going to try to help Mom and Dad as much as possible. I think maybe this year will bring changes, maybe some new boyfriends. Boys might finally start to take an interest in me. But I shouldn't count on it.
>
> A new year is beginning and I hope a new me is beginning also. I'm happy with the way things are. But here is a list of ten improvements I want: I don't want to be late for anything; I want to start thinking of others more, especially my parents; I want to make myself look the best in the mornings; don't gossip or talk about anyone, you're only likely to change your mind about that anyway; don't complain about things, especially to parents; trust and believe in yourself, have confidence; open up, don't be so shy; get things done, quit procrastinating; turn my lights out at eleven; stop nail-biting and leg-shaking.
>
> It was a fast year. I grew up a lot. I think I'm a lot more confident in myself than I was a year ago. Don't feel so inferior to a lot of people as I used to. I'm starting to look my age and feel it. But I still don't feel at ease with a lot of people; I tend to avoid them. I think the thing I'm most happy about is that I've decided I don't need certain friends of mine. Claire and Lisa are the only ones I want as best friends. . . . I'm so glad to have people who care about me as much as my family, Bobby, Lisa and Claire do. How many people have friends they can really trust?
>
> This next year I'm going to pray every morning for help, reach out to others, and let nothing get me down.

The fact of the matter was, Mary began the new year with more friends than a lot of her classmates. She belonged to three close-knit cliques consisting of six girls each. She had a couple of "best-friend" relationships and a boyfriend. Hundreds of students knew her by name. So she was hardly the outcast she sometimes felt herself to be.

Beginning the very first day of 1979, Mary started making regular entries in The Complete Runner's Day-by-Day Calendar, *a special diary designed for runners to keep track of their mileage. She used it for that purpose and as a record of feelings about life, school, friends, and feelings.*

I wanted to be more disciplined about my running during 1979. My new diary would force me to be diligent, because each page had a place for me to list mileage. Any day I didn't run I would have to write in a zero or leave the line blank, thereby admitting and recording my failure. Vowing to keep the zero days to an absolute minimum, I set a year-long goal to run three thousand miles.

Either the extra incentive really worked or I developed discipline, because in January—the toughest month of the year for training—I ran an average of seven miles a day, almost every day. And for the first time in my life I worked out with weights four times a week.

My first competitive test of the new year and my new determination came on February 3 when I ran in the Cherry Blossom Pre-Race. I finished second to Elaine Yurek, a woman in her late twenties who had been a primary force in women's roadracing around the area for a couple years. But what bothered me even more than another defeat was that the anxiety that plagued me earlier in my running career seemed to have returned.

My diary tells of my disappointment:

> I ran a race today. Elaine Yurek passed me and I got sick. It looks like I'm going to have a terrible season, unless I start working. What happened to the tough runner I used to be? It's going to change. Even if I die.

Once again I tried to pick up my training pace. And the week ending March 4, I ran sixty-five miles. Later in the month I won a special pre-race over the Cherry Blossom Run course and began to feel that my hard work might pay off. But after a poor finish at an indoor meet early in the track season, I decided I still wasn't doing enough. I told my coach, "I'm going to start running twice a day. That's what it's going to take to improve on my nineteenth-place finish in states."

Every morning before school I ran five miles. Then after school I did the regular workout with the track team. With the extra work I began to feel my strength building. And each week, as I filled in the line in my running diary for "Weight," I noticed a drop—from 105 pounds down to 101.

On April 19 I ran a 5:07, a new personal best, in a 1-mile race. But when I reported the results in my diary, I wrote: "I won't be happy until I break five minutes."

At the end of the month I finished first among the women for my second straight Cherry Blossom Run title. In my diary I reported:

> I almost didn't run the race because my knee hurt. But I didn't do too bad. Felt tired at the end. I need more strength.

A few days later I looked at my yearly goal of three thousand miles and assessed my performance of the preceding week during which I'd run sixty-eight miles.

> Terrible mileage. I'm depressed. I feel raunchy, like I'll never do it if I don't get my mileage up.

Once more Mary increased her mileage until she was running seventy-six miles a week in May. But a track season full of victories nearly came to a disappointing end when two days before the district meet, she came down with the flu and a 102-degree fever. But on May 15 she amazed herself and her coach by running well enough to bring home first-place medals in the mile and the 2-mile.

Though she had convinced herself that she shouldn't set her goals too high, the ultimate goal of a state championship seemed closer than ever. Because she had turned in the best times in the state during the track season, she went into the state finals seeded first in the 2-mile race for her division—Class AA schools. And the word around Meyers High the week before finals was "Mary's number one in the state." This time she wasn't the only one expecting a win.

The race started at a much faster pace than I wanted. Marya Small, a girl from Philadelphia, took off and I had to follow. For seven laps she kept the lead as I hung back in second, waiting for her to tire and wondering as to the whereabouts of Donna McClain, the other runner in contention for the lead. *You've got to stay close to Marya and keep pushing to stay ahead of Donna,* I kept telling myself. Then, in the eighth and final lap, I tried to make my move on Marya. But she had a strong kick left and I just couldn't seem to catch her. I didn't think Donna was far behind, but I made it a practice never to look back. So when the crowd noise began to swell as I approached the finish, I didn't know what was happening. Then I heard thundering footsteps and Donna burst past on my right and crossed the finish in second place, to the wild cheers of the crowd applauding her effort.

Not even slowing down at the finish, I kept running right out of the stadium where I finally threw myself down on a grassy slope and cried. *I'll never win a state championship. All that work this year, and now this. Why couldn't I have at least made a run for second? Why did I let that girl pass me at the end?*

For two hours my family and friends searched the field and the stands for me. Bobby finally found me sitting and crying on that little hill and tried to cheer me up. "Mary," he said, "you have to look at this realistically. You're only a sophomore. You've got two more chances at the state championship. You'll win it eventually."

I was inconsolable. I didn't want to wait another year and no words could soothe my disappointment. But I was able to halt the tears and make it back to the stadium for the awards ceremony. I tried in vain to force a smile as I stood on the third step of the awards platform and accepted my medal. But when I reached over to congratulate the girls who stood on the two steps above me, I didn't mean it.

I blew it. And there were only two years left to win the state championship.

Chapter 5

In the months that followed, what Bob's words couldn't do after that championship race, his presence and special attention did. Just being with him gave me a soul-deep sense of assurance. He made me feel accepted. Loved.

We spent a world of time together that summer between my tenth and eleventh grades, much of it at his family's place on Harvey's Lake. We would lie on the floating swimming dock for hours, soaking up the sun. But Bob's presence, his caring, gave me a greater feeling of warmth and well-being than an entire summer of solar rays.

Bob now had a driver's license, so we had the new freedom of mobility. We double-dated a lot with some cross-country friends, but we also had a lot of time to ourselves to take in a movie or just to eat out and talk. Many evenings we would drive out to Harvey's Lake and take long, quiet canoe rides in the cool of the evening. Sometimes we would talk, sometimes just drift, listening to the peaceful lapping of the water on the bow and relishing the sounds of nature and our own shared silence.

Since I wasn't yet sixteen, I couldn't find a summer job. So I had three whole months to devote to Bob and to training. I hated working out with weights, but David kept telling me I would have an extra edge on the competition with increased upper-body strength. So I pumped more iron on the homemade bench press

David rigged up and even added to the mileage I'd been running during track season.

On July 5, I totaled up the previous week's mileage to discover I'd run a hundred miles. Although I felt pleased with my running effort, I figured I could put out more in other areas. And I wrote in my diary, "Need to be doing extra sit-ups."

Despite the extra training, when I recorded my weight in my running diary on July 7, I found I had reached an all-time personal high. But I just jotted down the numbers without really stopping to think about it.

The next day, however, I turned to the diary page for July 8 and saw a photograph of a young runner who eventually became an Olympic medal winner. Under her picture there appeared this caption: "If you want to run well, don't be satisfied with normal weight. Top runners are almost always underweight. Says one, 'If you don't look gaunt, you're out of shape.'"

I looked back at the weight line I'd filled in the day before: 107. And I said to myself, *I'm certainly not gaunt.*

I had never worried about my weight. It had naturally fluctuated between 100 and 105 all the years I'd been running. I ate whatever I felt like eating, including junk food, because I knew I'd run the calories off. So I probably would have shrugged aside the slight weight gain and the quote about being gaunt if it hadn't been for a number of other incidents that summer.

One afternoon I stood in the kitchen with a stack of Oreo cookies in one hand and a big glass of milk on the counter of the breakfast bar when David walked in. "You better be careful what you eat, Mar," he said. "If you don't watch it, you'll put on weight and it'll slow you down."

My first reaction was defensive. "Don't worry about it. I run it all off."

"I don't know, Mar," he bantered. "I think your thighs may be getting a little heavy."

"They are not!" I snapped, quickly downing the remainder of my afternoon snack. But a few minutes later I stood in front of the mirror in my room, studying my legs. I had matured some and developed more of a figure over the preceding year. Yet even at a top weight of 107, with my height of 5′4″, I told myself, *I'm not too heavy.*

My brother's off-hand comment planted another concern deep in a corner of my mind. But I kept telling myself, *As long as I keep training, I've got nothing to worry about.* And I did train. Too much for the liking of Coach Watkins who called me about the middle of July and told me he wanted me to take a break and get some rest. He didn't want me to burn out before cross-country season started.

I took off the week of July 16, running only twenty-two miles that week. That seemed like enough rest to me. The next week I was back up to seventy miles.

One reason Mary kept working so hard was because she wanted to make a good impression at two different running camps she planned to attend later in the summer. The first one, a pre-Olympic training camp starting on August 6 at Lehigh University, included top women runners from throughout the northeast. Mary had qualified for an invitational with her impressive showing during her sophomore track season. But the camp turned out to be something of a disappointment.

It wasn't until I arrived at Lehigh that I realized how few distance runners would be there. I felt like turning around and going home when I learned we'd be subjected to a variety of track skills tests during the first couple of days. The coaches kept charts of all our results in events such as the shot put (I embarrassed myself), the 50-yard dash (I had the slowest time in camp), and the hurdles (I didn't even run them). And while everyone else eagerly compared their scores, I kept to myself and wondered, *Why can't we do something where I can prove myself?* I knew if only we'd take a 10-mile run I could beat anyone in camp.

One evening at Lehigh, a state-university track coach lectured on the subject of weight. "You girls have to be careful now as you're maturing," she said. "I've lost so many runners who've ruined their careers by putting on weight. If you don't keep your weight down now, it'll only get worse when you graduate high school and start college."

I had always assumed I could put off these warnings about weight gain until college. But here was an expert saying I needed to worry about it now. And I began to look around me. All the girls on the Penn State team were skinny sticks. Maybe I needed to pay more attention to my weight.

One of the girls I ate with regularly told me she was on a diet. Another girl, seeing my heaping plate of food, commented, "You sure do eat a lot."

I began to feel so self-conscious that I wondered if there was something wrong with my appetite. My insecurities were exaggerated by my poor showing in the skills tests and my feelings of physical awkwardness.

Plus, I met Ceci Hopp, one of the few distance runners in camp. She had been Connecticut state champion in cross-country and the mile. She looked like a model with long blond hair reaching almost to her waist. She always dressed as if she had just jogged off the pages of some sports fashion magazine; she wore colorful new running suits provided by a sports-clothes manufacturer, while I ran in faded old sweats. In addition to her beauty, Ceci had also been blessed with the gracefulness of an accomplished ballet dancer—which she was. When the coaches videotaped our running, they showed Ceci's tape and told the rest of us, "Now that's perfect running form."

That night I wrote in my diary: "I thought the videotapes were helpful. But I looked too heavy compared with the other girls. I'm cutting out all the in-between snacks. And only one ice cream a day."

But I left camp feeling like no one there thought much of my ability.

It was a different story the following week, however, at the Blue Mountain Sports Camp in the Pocono Mountains. At this special camp exclusively for cross-country runners, Mary had a chance to show herself a standout among the 150 boys and girls who attended.

Unlike the pre-Olympic camp, everything we did at the cross-country camp was geared for distance runners. I did so well in the preliminary trials that the coaches allowed me to run with the boys—the only girl in the pack.

I thrived on the recognition I received as the toughest female runner in camp. And while running with the boys, I could relax and not worry about competition. All I had to do was run. And run.

I ran four miles every morning, six miles in the afternoon over rough terrain, and another couple miles of intervals around a field. And some nights I would go out for another run that would bring my total up to eighteen miles for the day. After one day of four workouts, I wrote in my diary: "I'm starting to get in shape. But I need more work on my movement and my breathing when I'm tired."

One day early in my second week of camp, the hard running up and down rough terrain finally took its toll in the form of a huge blood blister on the back of my right heel. I tried to cushion it with tape and gauze, but when it burst I had no choice but to hobble to the infirmary. As the nurse cleaned out the blister and patched me up, I thought dejectedly, *There goes my mileage for this week.*

But after an evening of limping around camp, my spirits and determination were back up enough for me to tell my diary: "I am going to run in the morning. I'm going to try for twenty miles tomorrow."

By the time camp concluded, I felt better than ever about my chances for a great junior-year cross-country season. But the summer's experiences had also sensitized me to the issue of weight.

On August 29, because I didn't do my morning run, I consciously limited my calorie intake for the first time in my life. I ate only 1700 calories that day, even though I ran thirteen miles later.

Since a person's body burns about 100 calories for each mile run, Mary didn't have much nutrition left after running to fuel her regular daily routine. But Mary wasn't really thinking through the implications; she was merely responding to her new weight concerns.

Mary's running diary contained another quote that reinforced her concern when she read it near the beginning of school: "Researchers studying navy pilots who spent time in Vietnamese prisoner of war camps were startled to discover that the former POW's were healthier than servicemen who hadn't been captured. The reason was that once imprisoned, the POW's fell to their ideal weight and ate a diet low in cholesterol and fats. For runners, the lesson is clear."

What was even clearer in Mary's mind was that running and eating were somehow connected. It was as if they were two opposing weights at opposite ends of the scale. And she had become convinced that when she reduced the running on one end, she needed to reduce the food intake on the other to keep her weight in balance. What Mary didn't realize was that her rigorous summer of training was taking a heavy physical toll.

The first week in September I took first in a 3-mile run, and in cross-country I got off to a great start for the season. I won every league meet and numerous invitationals around the state. Whenever I ran, I felt in the best shape I'd ever been. And yet I felt exhausted. I often walked into class late simply because I couldn't muster enough energy to hurry through the halls.

One day, as I shuffled into history class sometime after the final bell, my teacher got a big laugh from the class when he asked me, "Mary, how can you run so fast and walk so slow?"

I didn't answer. But I told myself the problem was my daily routine that started with a 6:00 A.M. run and didn't end until I wrapped up all my homework—often after midnight. "I've got to get to bed earlier," I told my diary on several occasions. But habitual tiredness seemed a reasonable price to pay for my best cross-country season ever and another term of honor-roll grades.

I capped off my most enjoyable running season of my career at the end of October with my third class-AA district cross-country championship in as many years. This district championship wasn't tainted by finishing behind a class-AAA runner. Cheryl had graduated and I was now the best female high-school runner in the valley. And I proved it to everyone by crossing the finish line two whole minutes ahead of the next finisher.

The Meyers High School boys' cross-country team won the state championship the next week. I was thrilled for Bob and all the other guys I had been running with for years. And the joy of their victory softened the blow of another disappointing third in yet another state championship race for me. Once more I wrote in my diary: "I should have gotten second . . . now there's only one more chance left for a state cross-country championship."

The boys' team celebrated their victory and quit training. But I continued my daily workouts to compete in two post-season events—the Junior Nationals and the Junior Olympics. I ran one of the worst races of my career in the Junior National meet held in North Carolina over Thanksgiving. More than forty girls finished ahead of me—I had no idea the national competition would be so tough.

The Junior Olympics nationals the next week went much better. I finished a surprising fourth. Ceci Hopp took first. But even though I hadn't expected to do so well, I still didn't collapse at the finish. So I wrote in my diary that I "should have run harder."

Still, I'd had enough success in cross-country to feel as if I could take some time off. From December 10 until December 23 I didn't run at all. And I felt only mildly frustrated on the last day of the year when I totaled up twelve months worth of mileage to discover I'd fallen a hundred miles short of my 3000-mile goal for the year.

That Christmas proved to be the happiest of my life. Mostly because of Bob. We took a gorgeous sleigh ride through the snow-blanketed mountains. He gave me a new pair of ice skates on Christmas Day, and we spent most of the remainder of our vacation breaking them in. We would skate for hours in the crisp, invigorating cold before heading indoors for hot chocolate, cookies, and the comfortable warmth of each other's company.

Despite the disappointments, the school year was going great. Not only had I achieved more running success than ever, but I had Bob again. And I had the privilege of sharing in the excitement and the honors of his senior year. Not only had he been part of the boys' cross-country team that took first place in the state, he had also made all-state in band and had been named a National Merit Scholarship semi-finalist. That someone so special cared about me seemed more wonderful than a dream.

And it made me more determined than ever to prove myself worthy of his love.

Mary trained hard through the winter. And when spring arrived she started junior-year track season running strong. Before midseason she was turning in better times than she had at season's end the year before when she had been seeded first in the Pennsylvania Interscholastic Athletic Association championships. Her weight was fluctuating normally between 105 and 101. And the long-time dream of a state championship once again consumed her thoughts. Until disaster struck.

One day near the end of April I was running up a hill on a golf course with some of my track teammates when I felt a stabbing pain in the back of my knee. I staggered to a stop and waited for the sensation to subside. But it didn't. So I hobbled back to school. The longer the pain lasted, the more concerned I was that it was something worse than a cramp.

The coach told me to stay off the leg for a couple days. But I ran anyway. One doctor called it a lateral hamstring pull; another diagnosed the injury as a torn tendon. Both of them said I would have to quit running until it healed.

I did take a few days off, but we were in the middle of track season. So I tried the leg again. The pain was too great, and I was forced to miss the remainder of the regular track season. The doctors said I wouldn't do any permanent damage by running on the leg, so I took a cortisone shot two days before the district championship and competed with a bandaged knee.

I couldn't do any better than second in the mile. But I outlimped the field to win yet another district championship medal in the 2-mile run. Even so, standing on the victory stand to receive my medal, I knew districts would have to be my last race of the year. My sense of disappointment was best expressed in an article by a sports columnist for the *Wilkes-Barre Times Leader* who wrote the following, two days before the state track and field championships:

> Friday was supposed to be one of the biggest days of the year for Mary Wazeter. Friday was supposed to be the day the Meyers High School track standout vindicated five months of grueling workouts. Friday was the day she proved the end invariably justifies the means. Friday was supposed to be the day.
>
> But for the Mohawk distance runner, the initial day of the PIAA state competition will take on a different air.
>
> Because when the gun goes off for the Class AA 3200-meter event on the campus of Shippensburg State College, she'll be just another member of the large crowd in the stands. . . .
>
> Wazeter, who finished third in the 3200 at the state meet last year and who scored another third last fall at the state cross-country meet, was convinced this year's PIAA meet would have been better.
>
> "If everything went right, I think I could have finished in the top three. The girl that won it last year I beat in cross-country."
>
> But everything did not go right. And the Meyers junior suddenly was faced with another decision—whether or not to attend the state meet in any capacity.
>
> "At first, I didn't want to go. I didn't think I could take that. The whole year, all I've been thinking about is states, states. They're

the two biggest days of the year. I've been waiting since January. I can't believe I'm not going. I'm going to try not to think about it.

"But it's not going to be easy."

Friday may be the most difficult day of Wazeter's athletic life.

It wasn't easy to sit on the first row of the stands and watch. "I can't believe it. I can't believe it. I can't believe it," I kept saying over and over to Bobby, who sat beside me. He tried to console me just as he had the year before. But I couldn't quit thinking, *Another whole year before I can stand on that starting line.*

I rode home telling myself, "You've only got one year left to become a winner." But in the meantime, I knew I had a long period of enforced inactivity.

And remembering the weight warnings from the previous year, I knew that for the first time in my life, I was going to have to carefully monitor everything I ate.

Chapter 6

Late one afternoon I found Mom puttering around the kitchen when I went in for a snack.

"Do you think I'm getting heavy?" I asked her.

"Oh, I don't know, dear," she replied absent-mindedly as she rummaged through a cupboard. "But you're certainly not thin."

Thin was what I wanted to be, though. And I set my goal to be down to 100 pounds for the junior-senior prom. I began to count calories. Carefully planning exactly what I would eat each day became an early-morning ritual. And as my weight dropped from 105 to 104 to 103, I thought, *This isn't going to be hard at all.*

The day before the prom I stepped on the scales to discover I still had one pound to go. So I went through the usual school routine without eating a thing all day. And the next day, after twenty-four hours of fasting, I reached my goal.

That evening I walked proudly into the school gym on Bob's arm. My dress—a pink chiffon, form-fitting formal—fit perfectly. My figure looked just the way I wanted it. Better still, it felt good to have achieved the goal I had set for myself. Though some of the frustration of track season remained, I was happy. I had a date with a handsome boy I really cared about—a boy who cared for me. Since he was vice-president of the student-faculty council, everyone knew Bob. He belonged and I was with him, so I felt I belonged. We were sharing a wonderful evening with a group of friends and classmates. And for the first time in a long time, I was satisfied with my life.

Keeping my weight down proved to be a bigger challenge, however. I cut my intake down to a carefully monitored 1200 calories a day—a limit set after careful, logical calculations. My traditional training diet had consisted of approximately 2200 calories, but I had been running an average of ten miles a day, which burns roughly only about 1000 calories. Now that I wouldn't be able to run for a few weeks, I could only maintain my pre-prom weight loss by sticking to a 1200-calorie daily regimen.

Mealtimes weren't so bad. I'd eat a piece of toast for breakfast and maybe an apple or an orange for lunch. For supper, I would eat small portions of whatever Mom fixed. The real temptation came right after school. Without my afternoon run, I had nothing to do. I didn't want to watch TV, and after spending all day in school, I didn't feel much like reading. What I really wanted to do was eat. A stack of Oreos and milk. Or a heaping bowl of chocolate chip ice cream. The refrigerator seemed like a giant magnet, drawing me to the kitchen. Most afternoons I resisted.

But during those last few days of my junior year I began to realize how structured my high-school life had been—and what a big part eating played in that structure. I had always considered food as the fuel for running. But after seeing the daily struggle it took to stay out of the refrigerator after school, I began to think perhaps running was a rationale for eating. Again, I wondered just how overweight I would be if I were not a runner. But that question only intensified my determination to hold the line on my weight.

That new determination helped me successfully fight the weight battle despite the rash of year-end celebrations, and prompted me to vow, *I'm not going to eat anything,* as I dressed for the big graduation party Bobby's family was giving him.

I arrived at his house a little late in hopes of avoiding some of the food. But it was no use. Food covered every flat surface in sight. I hadn't been there five minutes when Bob's mother asked, "Mary, aren't you going to get a plate?"

"Later," I replied.

I spent the evening laughing and talking with Bobby's friends and family, admirably playing the part of the happy girl friend of the guest of honor. I tried to block out the food by looking people directly in the eye as we talked. But often I would catch myself subconsciously tuning out their voices as my attention shifted to the feast-filled tables. I would snap myself out of my reverie, but before long someone would recount a funny incident from geometry class and my eyes would focus on a giant bowl of chip dip. In the middle of explaining to one of Bob's aunts that I had another year of high school to go, I'd catch a mouthwatering whiff of smoked ham and have to remind myself of my resolve: *Not one bite, Mary.*

But the more determined my control, the more I focused on the food. Even the sound of people chewing made me think about food. Yet I didn't give in. When everyone left at the end of the party, I still hadn't taken a bite. That night I went to bed, hungry and exhausted from my big emotional battle. But I had won!

Though pleased with my self-discipline, I also felt a shiver of apprehension. The food at that party had seemed so appealing to every one of my senses that I had been afraid the smallest taste would mean a total loss of control. I hadn't been able to eat one bite without fear that I'd try to eat a truckload. Food had become an enemy, waiting to devour *me.*

Summer's change of schedule made things a little easier. Two part-time jobs kept Mary busy and out of the house much of the time. During the middle of the day, she worked as a lifeguard at the Holiday Inn. Late afternoons and evenings she worked at a local health and fitness spa, where the owner, who had followed her running career in the newspapers, hired her over thirty other applicants. He had really wanted someone who could help lead some vigorous exercise classes, but Mary couldn't manage those with her slow-healing knee. So he made some adjustments in his staff schedule and let her do clerical work, give the quickie tours, and explain the membership plan to visitors interested in joining the club. Another part of her job was regularly weighing and measuring members and recording any progress in their weight-loss plans.

Mary was so engrossed in her own struggle to maintain her weight that monitoring the weight of others prompted some unusual emotional responses. On the one hand, every time she pulled the tape measure around the waist or thigh of some overweight matron, she felt a little superior, taking pride in her discipline. At the same time, she couldn't measure a bulging tummy or a flabby thigh without lecturing herself sternly: I could look like this if I weren't a runner.

So her work at the spa reinforced Mary's concern about counting calories. It made her even more anxious to train again. In the meantime she had to rely on upper-body workouts at the spa and a mile's worth of laps in the swimming pool every day to keep her muscles toned.

In addition to my workouts, I religiously counted calories. If I ate more than my usual allotment for lunch, I would eat a smaller-than-usual supper. It was control at any cost!

One weekend my brother Gerry brought his girl friend home to meet the family. The next thing I knew, Dad was calling us all together.

As I came down the stairs, he urged, "Hurry and get ready, Mary. We're going out for dinner tonight."

Halfway down, I stopped. "I can't go."

"Why not?"

"I ate a sandwich for lunch."

"So?"

"So, I've already had a thousand calories today and I can't afford to eat supper."

"That's ridiculous."

"It's not ridiculous, Dad. I'm not going to eat supper. Just go on without me."

With each exchange, we upped the volume another notch.

"Mary," Dad said, determination edging his voice. "Gerry is here with his girl friend, and we're all going out as a family to eat together. We don't have to have a big scene."

"I don't want a big scene either. I just don't want to go."

"Then go for the rest of us."

"I don't want . . ."

"Mary! You're going."

"Okay. But I don't plan to eat anything."

Dad had reached his limit. "Then stay here by yourself. But you'll have to do your own explaining to your brother."

I conceded defeat and trudged out to the car, with Mom's whispered reassurance in my ear: "You don't have to order a whole meal." But I was afraid I couldn't restrain myself. And the whole idea of being forced to go made me angry.

I hoped my silence seemed more like shyness than sullenness to Gerry and his friend. I even ordered a meal that came with a free trip to the salad and dessert bars. Food seemed to be an all-or-nothing proposition for me, and that night it was all. When Mom cheerfully commented, "You're having a pretty big dinner for someone who wasn't hungry," I maintained a frustrated silence. But when we got home I ran straight to the bathroom and stepped on the scales.

For the most part, my family accepted my diet. Mom fixed a lot of nonfattening dishes for me. And though she and Dad sometimes asked if I was eating enough, they didn't seem overly concerned.

When Judy came home for a summer visit, she noticed right away. "You've lost some weight, haven't you?" she asked.

I proudly informed her that I weighed only 98 pounds and was holding steady.

"You're eating sensibly, aren't you? You're not starving yourself?"

"No, of course not," I assured her, making a mental note to

eat enough during her visit to forestall any fears she might have about me.

"That's good. Because you're looking great, Mary," she said. Her encouraging response gave me another boost of resolve that lasted long after she had gone back.

As the summer progressed I tried hard not to make a big deal out of my diet around Bobby. But if I knew we were going to be eating out on a date, I purposely didn't eat a thing all day so I could have a normal meal with him. On the weekends we spent a lot of time at Harvey's Lake where my uncle and Bobby's folks had summer cottages. I would skip lunch to swim lap after lap between the two docks, trying to burn up any excess calories. Then I would lie in the sun and daydream about food until evening when I would pig out on barbecued chicken, steaks, or hamburgers.

Sometimes I scared myself with the amount I could eat after going a full day without food. And when I was still hungry after one of our dates, I would come home and scavange anything edible I could find in the refrigerator. That scared me more.

Although the cycle of fasting and feasting disturbed me, something else bothered me. As Bob and I ate pizza with friends after a movie or gnawed on ribs with his family at the lake, I would concentrate so hard on what I was eating—the taste, the aroma, the texture—that I couldn't carry on an intelligent conversation. Sometimes I wouldn't even hear what Bob was saying to me. And that scared me most of all.

What's wrong with me, I would ask myself as I lay in bed at night. *Do I really care more about food than I do about people? Why is this happening to me? If Bob knew what was happening, he wouldn't have anything to do with me.*

I just wanted to keep my weight under control while I was temporarily out of training. But somehow food had become an obsession.

In fact, Mary was so concerned about her strange compulsion that when she saw a newspaper notice about an Overeaters Anonymous group meeting scheduled one evening at her mom's church, she decided to go. When she invited her mom to go along, Edith Wazeter reacted with surprise. But when Mary confessed that she couldn't stop thinking about food and that she was afraid something was wrong with her, Mary's mother quickly consented.

I felt strong but mixed emotions as Mom and I walked into the First Presbyterian Church. I hoped to find release from my eating problems, but also dreaded the thought of talking about such personal feelings with a bunch of strangers. If Mom hadn't been with me, I would have chickened out.

The OA chapter met in the church parlor. As we took our seats and waited for the meeting to begin, I surveyed the other people. My first panicky reaction was "I don't belong here!" I was the youngest and thinnest person in the room. Most of the people were women—many so huge they could have used two chairs.

Finally, a woman stepped to the front and introduced herself. "I'm Sarah, and I'm a compulsive overeater." And then she went on to tell about how she had been controlled by food until she had been able to change some of her patterns of eating and regain some control through the help and encouragement of friends in OA.

Then another person stood and said, "I'm Alice, and I'm a compulsive overeater."

As one after another spoke, I found myself identifying with their attitudes, their fears, their emotions toward food. When it was my turn to speak, I reluctantly stood. "Hi, I'm Mary, and I'm a compulsive overeater."

I told about my pattern of fasting and then stuffing myself. I talked about my frustration and my feelings of guilt that I couldn't eat normally. And everyone in the room listened respectfully to every word I said. After the meeting many of the people introduced themselves to me. A couple gave me phone numbers and told me to call anytime, day or night, when I felt I was going to gorge myself with food.

As I walked out of the meeting among all those huge overstuffed bodies, I scolded myself, *Maybe you do belong here, Mary. If you hadn't run off so much of what you've eaten in your life, maybe you'd be a blimp too.*

Shortly afterward, the doctor gave me the okay to test my knee with a little running. "Don't run if you feel any pain at all," he instructed. So I jogged for a couple days toward the end of July. Then I decided to try a longer, more leisurely run through town with one of my teammates. Everything felt great the first mile or two. But just as we were running through the downtown area, a pain shot through my leg and I collapsed. I stood up and tried to walk it off, but I could only manage to hobble to the front steps of the Jewish Community Center and wait for my friend to call my dad to come pick me up.

There on the steps, with traffic and sidewalk pedestrians moving steadily all around me, I cried. I wasn't crying because of the pain in my leg, but because it was almost August, near the start of cross-country training for my senior year of high school. And my knee still hadn't healed.

A year before, I'd been running sixty, seventy, and more miles a week just to get in shape for training. But now, just shy of a month before the start of the season, I could barely walk. This was my final season and all my hopes of a state championship in cross-country now seemed an impossible dream.

Chapter 7

A consultation with another doctor brought both good and bad news. The good news was that there was no new damage to the knee. The bad news was that I was going to have to build the leg up gradually. And it was already time to begin hard training for cross-country.

I didn't know how I could be ready for competition by the first of September. But I began to run again, slowly—only two or three miles a day during early August. By the middle of the month, I had worked up to six or seven miles.

Toward the end of the month, I spent a few days with Bob's family at the lake. After we ran together the first day, Bob said, "You're doing better than you think, Mar. You're tiring me out. I don't think you're that far out of shape."

That was the first day I had pushed myself enough to believe I still had it in me to run my senior year. And some of my eating concerns began to ease up. I could even eat breakfast every day with Bob's family.

The time at the lake with Bob was bittersweet. Since these were our last days together before he headed for college, we relived a lot of wonderful memories, trying not to look ahead to a year apart.

One tough decision—one that I agreed to only because I didn't want to tie Bob down his first year in college—was to date other people. His glib assurance, "So many other guys will want to date you, Mar," reminded me of a similar promise he had made in tenth grade. I still didn't believe him.

By the opening of school my times were still slow, but at least I was running normal training sessions without any pain in the knee. And my strange famine-to-feast eating pattern had nearly disappeared. I knew I had to eat more now to run, so fasting was unnecessary. Besides, being on the move again and out of the house, I had neither the time nor the opportunity to stuff myself.

I still wanted to keep my weight under a hundred pounds. I took special pride in having lost enough over the summer to drop from a size 5 to a size 3. And when school started and I experienced the usual envy over the popularity of some of my friends, I was able to tell myself, *They may be more popular, but I'm thinner.* In that realization I found consolation.

But weight was no longer my biggest concern. Running strength was now the prime consideration. I forced myself to quit counting calories (a hard habit to break), and began to concentrate on eating the right balance of food. Fear of overeating was replaced by a fear of not eating the right amount of the right foods.

My summer-long obsession with food had left its mark. And I now saw, more clearly than ever, the direct connection between eating and running. They were two weights on opposite ends of the scale. I lived in the middle where I struggled to maintain a balance. Although I tried my best to control them, they also controlled me.

I could no longer simply enjoy eating without analyzing my food. And I couldn't run without thinking about what I would eat after the workout. As I ran early in the morning, I visualized the bowl of cereal I could eat for breakfast when I got back to the house. And when I ran cross-country practice every afternoon, I wasn't concentrating on my form or my speed; I was wondering what Mom had planned for supper.

Perhaps running and eating demanded an inordinate amount of Mary's attention because nothing else did. Socially, she had a lot of adjustments to make during that fall of her senior year. Bobby was at college; so all the hours she usually spent with him—running, dating, visiting with his family—were now idle. Her friends were more involved than ever in student government, cheerleading, band, and other extracurricular activities. Her good friend, Lisa Richards, was elected president of the student council and nearly every one of Mary's circle of friends were either on the council or held class office.

Not even the cross-country team provided a familiar haven for Mary. The boys she had run with since seventh grade—the entire squad from the boys' state championship team of the season before—had all graduated. Mr. Watkins, the only coach she had ever run for, had decided to retire from coaching after his state championship season. While she was the oldest, most experienced runner on the team, Mary had to adjust to new friendships, new coaches, and new routines. And for the first time since seventh grade, she was asked to train with other girls who couldn't push her as hard as the guys always had.

My friends gloried in the activities of senior year. But I spent a lot of that fall feeling like a stranger, standing on the outside looking in.

I didn't even want to go to the homecoming football game. The experience would be too painful. Lisa, the Carrol twins who had run with me over the years, and a couple other girls from our regular lunch table had all been selected as members of the homecoming court. I knew they would be paraded around the stadium to the cheers of the crowd and then escorted out onto the field at halftime by the most popular boys in school. One of my friends would be crowned homecoming queen and take her honored place in the history of Meyers High School. I didn't even have anyone to sit with at the game.

I did go to the game—late. And it wasn't so bad. At least not as bad as the next evening when I went to the homecoming dance. Alone. And late again. I got there in time to hear the introductions of the boys who had been nominated for homecoming king. The girls from the queen's court escorted them out to take their places around the mock thrones at the end of the gym. Then the king was crowned and took his place beside the queen, where they received the admiration and applause of their subjects for the evening.

When the ceremony concluded, the music began. As couples moved out onto the floor and started to dance, I shrank back and surveyed the scene. Bouquets of balloons bloomed in bright colors, and twisted crepe paper streamers spilled over bench and bleacher, transforming the utilitarian space into a magical kingdom. The girls, most wearing corsages, floated in the arms of their handsome escorts.

I felt as invisible as Cinderella's fairy godmother at the ball. I melted into the nearest wall. The eyes of every person in that room were riveted on every other person. Not a single glance met mine. Apparently no one knew, or cared, that I existed. Though I was crammed into that gym with hundreds of people who knew my name, I felt more alone than I had ever imagined. I wished I had never come.

The one bright spot that fall was the cross-country competition. Not the training, but the actual races. I won all Meyers' dual meets and even took first in some big invitational meets. While my times were consistently slower than during my junior year, they steadily improved as the season progressed. But the summer layoff had cost me speed and stamina, and I spent the entire fall playing catch-up.

Bob and my brother David, who both attended Franklin Marshall College in Lancaster, regularly scanned the sports sections of the papers for news of any serious contender I might have to face in the finals. Even though they kept assuring me there was no one I needed to worry about, I feared some unknown, fast-improving underclassman who might surprise me at the state meet.

I took my fourth consecutive district championship—for the second year in a row, finishing more than two minutes ahead of the rest of the field. Yet my time didn't match the all-time district record I had set my junior year, so heading into my last high-school cross-country competition, I was justifiably worried. It was my final shot at the state championship, and I still wasn't in the kind of shape I had been in last year when I'd come away with only third place.

The week before the finals my dad drove me to Allentown to walk through the championship course. Seeing the terrain ahead of time might help me to plot my race. I needed any advantage I could get. As I walked down the last long straight toward the finish, I imagined myself in the race. *I have to win. If I don't . . .* I couldn't allow myself to consider the possibility.

The day of the race, my personal day of reckoning, finally arrived. It dawned clear and cold—cold enough to wear my old blue ski cap.

The boys ran first, but I was too nervous to watch. So I wandered over to a nearby amphitheater to be alone. As the 10:30 starting time neared, I jogged around the parking lot to loosen up until it was time to head to the starting line.

When the gun sounded I sprinted out with a few others ahead of the field of two hundred runners. After so many years of disappointment, my new strategy was to go for the lead right at the start and let everyone try to catch me. I wasn't going to get myself boxed in behind the leaders and maybe not be able to overtake them at the end.

By the time we had run the first four hundred yards, I moved into the lead and congratulated myself on the execution of my plan. *Now all you have to do is stay here.*

For a cross-country course, this one was fairly flat. It wound in and out of cornfields and proved a poor course for spectators. But David had brought a gang of college friends with him and stationed them strategically around the course. I could hear nearly continuous shouts of encouragement and reports on the rest of the field. "Keep it up, Mary. The next three runners are fifty yards back!" "Lookin' good, Mar. Two miles to go!" "You're halfway there, Mary, but Holly's moving up on you."

Holly Green, a year younger than I, was the runner who promised the toughest competition. I could hear her gaining on me. As we ran through a cornfield, she moved past me and took the lead by about five yards. I stayed right with her for a couple hundred yards. Then, as we came out of the cornfield onto a long grassy stretch, I summoned up some reserve and regained the lead.

For the next mile I ran in sheer fear of losing. I knew Holly was still behind me because I could hear her. Not only that, but David's booster squad was keeping me apprised of every move she made. As we came out of the last turn and headed into the final quarter-mile straightaway, I was still in the lead, but only by twenty-five or thirty yards.

The muscles in my legs protested with every stride. My lungs screamed for air. In front of me lay the finish line I had been running toward for five years.

The crowd lined both sides of the course and, as I ran down that funnel of people toward the finish, I could tell from their excited screams that Holly was right on my heels, no doubt gaining on me.

But I could also hear friends and family calling out my name. I kept on running—for them as well as for myself. I broke the tape less than four seconds ahead of Holly Green.

As the spectators cheered my victory, I scanned the crowd until I spotted David. Then I ran for him, threw my arms around his neck and cried as the rest of my family quickly gathered around. When I finally let go of my brother, whose face was split in an ear-to-ear grin, I reached to embrace my mom and dad. But I couldn't control my tears of joy. Never in my life had I felt such total happiness. Even stronger than the happiness was an almost overpowering sense of relief.

Later, at the awards ceremony, when I stood on the platform to accept my state championship medal and the congratulations of the girls who finished behind me, the tears once again trickled down my face even as I smiled for the cameras.

Mary's state championship earned her an invitation to enter the national high-school cross-country competition sponsored by Kinney Shoes. The regional meet for the top high-school cross-country runners from throughout the northeast was held in New York City's VanCortlandt Park just two weeks later.

Mary surprised herself by finishing a strong fourth in the region and thereby qualified as one of the top seven runners eligible for the Kinney National Cross-Country Finals in San Diego the second week of December. For once in her running career, Mary wasn't worried about whether or not she was going to win. The all-expense-paid trip to California and a chance to run against the very best high-school runners in the nation was more than Mary had hoped for.

My old campmate, Ceci, took first in the New York City regional. A couple of other girls I had run against at big invitationals were among the top seven. Most of them had made enough of a name for themselves that they were sponsored by one of the major shoe companies. For example, Nike not only provided Ceci with all the running shoes she needed, but outfitted her like a fashion model with a canary yellow running suit, complete with matching yellow rain gear. I ran the regional race in my Wazeter original—a pair of old blue sweat pants and a faded, tattered, yellow sweat shirt. So, in addition to feeling honored, I felt more than a little out of place to be photographed with the six other finalists after the New York regional.

A couple of days before the finals in San Diego, all seven of the northeastern qualifiers, along with seven boys who had qualified for the boys' finals, convened at Kennedy Airport in New York City. On our flight to San Diego I once again felt awkward and out of place.

When the flight attendant brought us a delicious full-course dinner, I dug in with enthusiasm—until I noticed the girl sitting next to me. She hadn't touched a thing on her tray.

"Aren't you hungry?" I asked.

"No. I'm on a diet. I need to keep my weight down," she confided as she pulled out a small container of tofu.

I glanced around at the other athletes. Only one other girl was eating the airline food. I finished my meal because I was hungry, but I felt terribly self-conscious. And that was just the first incident on the San Diego trip that forced me to think about my eating habits.

The day before the finals, the sponsoring committee held a fancy reception for all the athletes. The event was held aboard a ship in San Diego Bay. Piles of beautifully arranged fruit and sumptuous seafood covered long rows of buffet tables. The other runners milled about, talking among themselves, apparently ignoring the feast before them.

After waiting for what seemed like an eternity for someone to make the first move, I said, "Well, I don't know about anyone else, but if I'm going to run a race tomorrow, I need something to eat tonight." And I heaped my plate full. Yet seeing only a few other runners picking nervously at their food, I didn't feel free to go back for seconds. I waited until I got back to my room instead and devoured a leftover sandwich.

We raced on a course in Balboa Park. Ceci won the national championship. But I finished a surprising and satisfying seventh—good enough to qualify me as a first-team, All-American, cross-country runner.

Despite my pride, the flight back east with Ceci and a couple other girls who finished ahead of me gave me still more reason to think about my eating habits. Studying their lean, lanky frames and watching them skip the meal I was too hungry to pass up, I recalled my visits to the OA meetings a few months earlier. Again I wondered what my weight would be if I didn't run it off.

I returned home victorious to my family, my friends, and the local media. The combination of my state championship and the strong finish in the national championship brought a steady stream of letters from colleges wanting to talk to me about athletic scholarships. I even received an offer from Brooks shoes to outfit me with equipment and sponsor me in future races.

Finally, I congratulated myself, *you're a winner. All those years of running are beginning to pay off.*

I was suddenly a nationally ranked and recognized runner. But the trip to San Diego convinced me I needed to do even more to guarantee my future. If I could just get rid of a little excess weight by the time track season rolled around, there was no telling how good I could be.

Chapter 8

Ninety-five pounds seemed a reasonable goal.

It wasn't just the weight I wanted to change; it was the distribution of those pounds. As I matured, I had become bulkier through the upper legs and thighs. *Mary,* I told myself as I stood in front of the mirror, *you've got saddlebag thighs.*

I wanted legs like the girls I saw in the fashion and running magazines. Lanky, sinewy legs where you could see the muscle definition.

Since tenth grade, I had had a favorite pair of dressy jeans with flower designs on the pockets. In recent months they had become uncomfortably snug. When my mom noted the tight fit and said, "It looks like we need to get you another pair of good jeans, Mar," I quickly declined, seeing a practical, easily defined incentive for my diet. *If I can lose just enough weight to wear those jeans again,* I thought, *everything will be perfect.*

I knew December would be a tough time to begin a 1000-calorie a day diet. So I took a firm stance from the beginning, vowing I wouldn't eat one Christmas cookie during the entire holiday season. The first real test came early in the month at Meyers High School's traditional Senior Tea.

All the other classes got the afternoon off. But the seniors came back to school with their mothers for a talent show, followed by a reception and a chance to meet teachers and school administrators.

Since it was a fancy occasion, everyone dressed up. The guys wore suits and ties, while the girls came in party dresses. (I wore a red skirt I had just taken in.) We served our mothers from tables laden with elegant trays of cookies and large bowls of punch. I kept my mom's plate stocked with cookies and refilled her cup often. But I didn't dare sample a cookie myself.

No one seemed to notice my abstinence. Teachers who walked up to talk with Mom or with me would invariably ask about my trip to San Diego or inquire about my college plans. Most of the time I managed to keep my mind off the food by trying to stay engrossed in conversation.

The afternoon reminded me of Bob's graduation party. I left the tea completely exhausted by my effort at restraint. But I went home with my vow unbroken, encouraged by my self-discipline. If I could survive the Senior Tea, perhaps the rest of the holidays wouldn't be as hard as I thought.

Christmas day was probably the worst. Late in the morning I went down to Mom's church to help serve a special Christmas dinner to the homeless people of Wilkes-Barre. After a couple hours in the church kitchen, smelling the savory scents, I headed back home to our own big family meal of turkey and all the trimmings.

Dabbling at my food, taking slow deliberate bites in order to prolong the meal, I became extremely aware of everyone around me. Their plates were heaped full, and they shoveled it all in with enthusiasm and exclamations of appreciation for the cook. *My whole family eats too much,* I observed. And I renewed my determination to overcome both my heredity and the holiday temptation.

In spite of my determination, or maybe because of it, food became the focus of Christmas vacation.

One night Bob and I went out to a movie with another couple, old high-school friends of his. I skipped breakfast and lunch that day so I could eat normally on our date, without making an issue of my new diet. By the time the movie was over, I was famished.

But when the subject of food came up on the way to the car afterward, nobody seemed interested, and the consensus was that we head to Bob's place where we could listen to music and talk.

I was so hungry I felt listless. As we got into the car, Bob and his friends began catching up on college and news of other friends. I rested my head against the back of the seat and closed my eyes, tuning out for a few minutes until I heard Bob's voice. "Mar, are you okay?"

I opened my eyes and focused on the ceiling of the car. "I think I just want to go home," I said. "I don't feel very well."

"Are you sick?"

"Just tired—probably because I haven't eaten anything all day."

"Why not?"

I didn't want to go into a big explanation. Not then. Not with the other couple in the car. "I just didn't feel like eating."

"We'll stop and get you something to eat," Bob said, his key in the ignition.

"No one else is hungry. Why don't you just take me home?"

But he insisted. We stopped at a pancake shop where my three companions ordered coffee while I downed a stack of pancakes drenched in butter and syrup. Everyone talked and acted as if everything were normal. But I felt incredibly self-conscious, forcing myself to eat slowly rather than wolfing down my food.

In January I got even more serious with the diet. I knew from my experience of the previous summer that I could probably drop the weight pretty quickly. The challenge would be to maintain my strength and stamina at the same time. That's where training would come in. After taking the month of December off from regular running and workouts, I was ready to combine training with diet to reach my dual goal: thinner and stronger.

The first thing every morning I did a hundred sit-ups with a ten-pound weight behind my head. At 6:00 A.M. I hit the streets and ran for five miles. Then I'd return home for a breakfast of half a grapefruit or a small bowl of cereal, followed by a weight workout before school. For lunch I would eat a piece of fruit or sometimes a bowl of broth and a cracker. After school I ran again. Supper was as light as possible, with constant checks on the calorie counter to be sure my intake never exceeded 1000 calories. Consequently, the weight did drop in a hurry.

One morning near the end of January, I stepped on the bathroom scale. The pointer indicated "95." I was delighted to find I had reached my goal. But when I walked back to my room and stood in front of the mirror, I still saw too much thigh. *It's been easy so far,* I told myself. *If I can stick to my regimen just a few more weeks, I'll get rid of these thighs and be in perfect shape.*

Every morning Mary checked her weight and appearance in the mirror. The numbers slowly, but steadily dropped—94 pounds, 93, 92. Every day she noted her progress with satisfaction. And every day she decided to lose just a little more weight.

Not surprisingly, Mary's vigorous pattern of self-deprivation began to take its toll. The workouts that had always given her such feelings of satisfaction and accomplishment became laborious chores. Some days each step seemed to require super-human effort. The joy of running began to fade.

Mary disregarded the nagging doubts and told herself she just needed to build up her endurance at the lower weight. January wasn't supposed to be a hard training month anyway. She didn't need to worry about speed; she would just concentrate on building her stamina.

But as the days and weeks rolled by, Mary lost rather than gained strength. She turned down a couple offers to compete at indoor invitationals, rationalizing the decision by reminding herself that she had never enjoyed running on indoor tracks anyway. And she also began to avoid opportunities to resume her regular runs with her friend and fellow varsity runner, Mark, realizing that she wouldn't be able to keep up with him.

But rationalization and weakness weren't the only signs that Mary was developing a serious eating disorder.

One day during homeroom I began to shiver. I looked quickly around the room to see if anyone else had noticed that the heat had been turned off. But the kids were sitting there in shirt sleeves or lightweight sweaters, oblivious to the penetrating chill.

I walked over to the teacher's desk. "May I get a pass to go to my locker? I'm feeling a little cold."

"Sure, Mary," she replied. "Hope you're not coming down with something."

I wore my coat in class the rest of the day, and the next morning I put on heavier clothing. But I stayed cold all winter. Some days I sat in class wearing a sweater over my blouse, wool knee socks under my slacks, clutching my overcoat around me. But I never stopped shivering.

While I maintained my usual, active schedule—continuing to work at the spa on Friday night, trying out and making the cast of a new school play—I began to withdraw from my friends. I hardly ever went to basketball games. And even though I was in charge of the refreshments for the Key Club's semi-formal dance, I delegated the duties to some of the other kids and went home without even staying for the dance. I just didn't feel like socializing.

The social withdrawal made it easy to cover up my new diet. With no one to be accountable to, I could avoid the whole subject. I didn't even tell Bobby in my letters, deciding to surprise him the next time he was home on break.

Some nights, when I had already reached my calorie limit for the day, I even resorted to lying to my parents. "I don't think I'll have any supper tonight. After play rehearsal, some of the kids from the cast will be going out for pizza." But there was no pizza stop. And if there had been, I wouldn't have touched a slice.

At first I felt funny deceiving my parents. But it became easier to lie. *I know what I'm doing. There's no sense in worrying them about something they wouldn't understand.*

It wasn't as if people hadn't begun to notice the change in me. One day Mr. Watkins, my former coach, saw me and commented, "You're looking too thin, Mary. You need to put on some weight."

Another teacher, who hurried past me as I shuffled slowly down the hall, suddenly stopped and turned around. "Are you all right, Mary? You're a little pale."

But their concern was more than offset one day in homeroom. I was wearing my favorite jeans again when a girl named Kristine said, "Mary, aren't those jeans getting kinda baggy on you?"

I smiled and looked down. The jeans did indeed hang loosely around my legs. And right then was when I decided it was time to go shopping for some new clothes.

Mom and I found several things I wanted in the "pre-teen" section of a local department store. All the new pants I bought were size 3. I walked out of the store, feeling proud of my accomplishment and vowing never to buy anything larger than a size 3 ever again. At home I modeled the new clothes in front of the mirror. I had finally gotten rid of those saddlebags and my thighs looked almost like I wanted them to. *Almost,* I told myself, *almost.*

My parents didn't say much about my weight loss until they saw me in the drama club play.

"Mary, you looked absolutely gaunt on that stage tonight," my Dad said when we got home. I could hear the alarm in his voice. I knew a confrontation was brewing. "Do you really think you look good like that?"

"I finally have my figure the way I want it."

"You don't have a figure, Mary. You look like a skeleton!"

I wanted to argue but I bit my tongue. *Better to let him have his say and let it blow over.* But he went right on.

"It's time we put a stop to all this foolishness about dieting.

You're running again and you've never had to worry about your weight when you're running. You're not healthy."

I had to say something. "I feel fine."

"You're not going to have any strength left if you keep this up," he insisted. "It's time you started eating regularly again. Three meals a day."

Next morning Dad made sure I ate breakfast. He protested when I insisted on having skim milk on my cereal. But he seemed satisfied that I had eaten something and seemed determined to make sure I kept eating.

Despite his concern, I remained committed to my strategy. I felt sure that if I stuck to my diet, I could slowly rebuild my strength at my lower weight. So I would leave the table as soon as I thought Dad would let me, and ate as little as possible, no matter how hungry I felt. I drank diet soda till I thought I'd burst and chewed sugar-free gum until my jaws ached to keep my mind and my mouth off fattening temptations.

I did relax a little at the annual cross-country banquet at the end of January. But I knew I would, so I ran a total of thirteen miles that day just so I could enjoy the banquet without feeling guilty. I was mostly looking forward to the special dessert table piled with homemade goodies baked by the mothers. My mom had told me she was taking my favorite fruit squares, and after almost two months of total abstinence from sweets, I decided to splurge.

The banquet could have been a highlight in my athletic career. I was recognized for captaining the girls' cross-country team, for winning an unprecedented fourth district championship, for my fourth-place finish in the regional, and my first-team All-American finish at the Kinney Nationals. But I heard little of the acclamation. My thoughts and eyes strayed to those heaping plates of goodies. Even while the master of ceremonies lauded my accomplishments, I was far more aware of the fruit bars beckoning from the dessert table.

When the time came, I heaped my plate high. Lots of people

did, so I didn't feel particularly conspicuous. But one of my teammates did call attention to my heroic helping of dessert and laughingly asked, "How can you eat so much and stay so skinny, Mary?"

I didn't bother to answer.

Mom took the leftover fruit bars home after the banquet. She had no sooner put them on the kitchen counter than I picked up a couple and began nibbling. As we talked over the events of the evening, I ate one piece after another, until Mom exclaimed, "Didn't you get enough to eat at the banquet, dear?"

"I guess not," I replied, returning the last bar to the plate. At that moment I still felt as if I could have eaten a truckload. I couldn't imagine ever getting enough to fill the empty feeling inside. And the feeling scared me.

So the next day I had more reason than ever to go back on my 1000-calorie routine. As the days and weeks passed, however, I realized I wasn't gaining any stamina. I kept telling myself, *Give it time. Give it time.*

When word came in mid-February that the coaches wanted all would-be track participants to attend some preliminary trials and workouts, I didn't feel ready. But my time was up.

The day blew in, cold and windy. Most of the snow had been shoveled off the track. Only a few crusty patches remained, as newcomers and veterans alike huddled in the first rows of the stands to hear the coach's instructions. I knew the routine. After we loosened up, we would divide into groups to run sprints, quarter-miles, and then a longer distance. The idea was to see who seemed best suited for the different events.

My group lined up to run a quarter. That distance was like a sprint for me. But I hadn't run any sprints since before Christmas.

The whistle sounded and we were off. By the time I'd run a hundred yards, I felt as if someone had tied weights to my arms and legs. Teammates who had never outrun me before moved into the lead. A ninth-grader novice ran neck-and-neck with me for two hundred yards before pulling steadily away. By the time I completed the quarter-mile lap, I felt sick—both physically and emotionally. *What have I done?* I asked myself. But I knew the answer. For the first time since beginning my crash diet, I realized I'd made a big mistake. I only hoped it wasn't too late to correct the damage.

"You okay, Mary?" the coach asked as I fought to regain my breath.

"I don't feel very good today," I admitted. "Just didn't get much sleep last night."

"You don't look good, Mary. Why don't you go on home?"

"Okay," I conceded. "And I think maybe I'll go in to the doctor and get my blood checked."

I felt so scared that when I finally dragged myself home from practice, I walked right into the kitchen and confessed to my mother, "I can't run. I think something is wrong with me."

Girl Scout Mary in the fourth grade

Mary *(left)* proudly displays her ribbon from her first track meet, 1975, with her best friend Lisa DelBalso.

Mary *(right)* in costume for her part in *The Sound of Music,* spring 1976

Mary with "the guys" during her first year of cross country in seventh grade, 1976—"a new beginning"

Brother David—"I looked up to him and tried to emulate him"

Seventh grade. "The more I ran, the better I felt—almost as natural as walking."

Determined and strong, Mary wins the Cherry Blossom Run, a 5-mile race in Wilkes-Barre.

Mary with high-school coach Larry Watkins, October 1979

In the process of winning her fourth straight District Cross-Country Championship in 1980

Prom night 1980—"I wanted to weigh 100 pounds to wear that gown"

One year later, Mary is 10 pounds lighter—"Pain behind the smile."

Mary takes her place on the victory stand after finishing first in the State Championship race for the 2-mile, May 1981.

High-school senior, 1981

"Still hiding the pain within." Mary with a family friend, Mary Mesharer, June 1981

"In the midst of anorexia." Mary with brother Gerry, sister-in-law Sandy, and Mary's mom, June 1981

With the Warren Street teammates in Aruba, 1981

With friends in Aruba, June 1981

The start of the 5-mile Mary Wazeter Benefit Run, which attracted 800 runners, summer 1982—"The largest roadrace ever held in that part of the country"

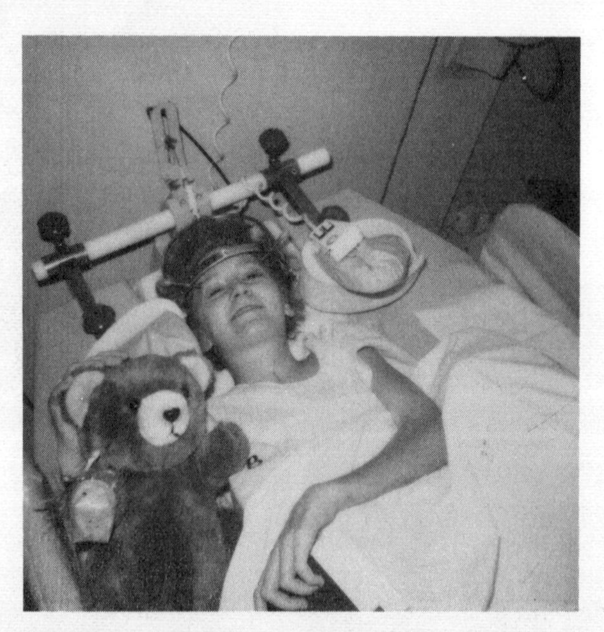

Mary on the Roto Rest Kinetic Treatment Table with her teddy, Warren, May to June 1982

Chapter 9

Mom hustled me to the bathroom and put me on the scales. "Eighty-nine pounds!"

I gave her the routine I'd been giving myself for weeks. "The scales must be broken."

"There's nothing wrong with these scales, Mary. No wonder you're weak! We need to get you to the doctor right away."

I didn't feel like protesting anymore. I knew I needed help.

Mom made the appointment and drove me to the doctor where I received a thorough physical. When the exam was over and the doctor called Mom into the office, we were both relieved to hear him say, "We found nothing at all wrong. Everything seems to be in order."

But I had mixed feelings when he added, "The reason for your weight loss is that you just haven't been eating enough for all the running you do. So, Mary, you're either going to have to cut down on the running or eat more. You need good nutrition to build back your weight and your strength."

"But I've been eating 1000 calories a day," I said.

He shook his head. "Don't worry about the number of calories. Eat whatever you want."

After months of zealous dieting, I was glad for medical permission to eat without guilt. But I couldn't shake a lingering fear that if I didn't maintain a habit of vigilance, my eating would careen out of control—like the night of the cross-country banquet. I would have to be extremely careful.

Mary's mom began preparing nutritious meals, rich in foods containing iron. And within a couple weeks Mary's weight had climbed back up to 95. But the speed with which she regained those first six pounds and the continued belief that she could do better in track at 95 pounds than she had at 105, convinced her that she ought not to gain another pound.

Mary's wariness was reinforced by almost every college recruiter who contacted her. And a lot of schools coveted her athletic talents.

While visiting the University of Pennsylvania, Mary was impressed with the lean frames of the female runners. And when the coach asked her weight, Mary proudly replied, "Ninety-five pounds." But the Penn campus seemed too big and spread-out to Mary; she couldn't imagine calling it home for four years. When the running coach from a major university in Florida called to talk to her about enrolling in his school, one of the first questions he asked was how much she weighed. And she couldn't forget the warning given by the Georgetown coach about the "freshman ten"—the weight gain of almost every incoming freshman.

Georgetown was one of two schools Mary was still considering early in that spring of 1981. The other was the University of Virginia.

Virginia had one of the strongest women's running programs in the country, having just won the women's national championship in the winter indoor season. Athletic competition would be tough there. At UVA, just making the seven-member cross-country squad would be a feat that, if accomplished, would put Mary among the country's top echelon of collegiate runners. So it was with great anticipation and interest that she accepted an invitation to visit the Virginia campus in March.

I arrived on the Charlottesville campus right in the middle of a women's track-team practice and watched the end of the workout as the team did sprints and finally jogged around the track to cool down. At the conclusion of practice, the coach introduced me to the other girls. I knew two of them who had been state champions in Pennsylvania. Since I had been sent a roster, complete with weights, I had already noticed that the top-ranked runners were the ones who weighed the least. So once again I felt pleased that I had been able to maintain my weight at 95 pounds.

After the girls had showered and dressed, I went with them to the dining hall for supper. No other students were left in the cafeteria by the time we got there, but they'd held one line open for us. The evening meal was Chinese food.

"I love Chinese food," I told the girl in front of me. But I didn't tell her how hungry I was. Traveling on the bus all day, I hadn't had a thing to eat since leaving Wilkes-Barre early that morning.

But I hadn't run any that day either, so I didn't want to eat too much. Nor did I want to look like a pig in front of the Virginia team. Using all the self-control I could muster, I forced myself to take only small servings. Even then, several members of the team took even less. One of the distance runners laughed when she saw me glance at her nearly empty plate. "Don't worry, Mary. I'm on a crash diet this week to get down to running weight by next week's meet."

After dinner a couple of the girls took me back to the room and talked more about the cross-country and track programs at UVA. Among the photos they showed me was a bunch of snapshots of the team party, given in honor of their national indoor championship. Pointing to a picture of several girls mugging for the camera from behind heaping bowls of ice cream, one of my hosts explained, "That was some victory celebration. First time most of us got to eat ice cream all year."

"Are you serious?" I asked.

"Yeah, the coaches watch our weight pretty closely here."

"What do you mean 'watch'?" I wanted to know.

"We have weekly weigh-ins to monitor our weight," one of

the girls explained. I made a mental note; apparently weight was as important as I had been led to believe.

The next day, I received the grand tour of the campus. I loved its old, colonial feel—right down to the rotunda designed by Thomas Jefferson himself. The school looked the perfect image of a college campus, with ivy-covered historic buildings and tree-lined walks. By the time I climbed back on the Greyhound bus and headed north for Pennsylvania, I was thoroughly impressed with the school.

My visit confirmed my impression that Virginia offered the best running program of any school I had considered. The competition and the coaches were tough, but I welcomed that kind of challenge.

The visit also confirmed the wisdom of my determination never again to let my weight get out of control—neither too high nor too low. UVA endorsed the "ideal weight" mentality, and I remained firmly convinced that 95 was ideal for me. I had only to keep training to rebuild my strength.

This conviction received a real test, however, the day of the spring's first track meet. Mom's cooking had put a few pounds on me, but I was still ten pounds under my state championship weight of the previous fall. And some of the race officials who hadn't seen me for almost six months expressed concern: "Have you been sick, Mary?" "How have you been, Mary? You look so thin." I tried to reassure them, but when it came time to run, I wasn't so sure.

I kept my sweats on as long as I could. With the chilly spring wind blowing right through me like a January blizzard, I felt as if I would freeze to death at the starting line of the mile run. When the gun finally sounded and I took off, it was the wind more than my opponents that impeded my progress on the track. When I wasn't running into the face of it, the stiff breeze threatened to push me off course from the side or to knock me down from behind. This natural element, which I'd never noticed before, now seemed my fiercest competitor.

By the third lap I was running on empty. Only the momentum that resulted from putting one foot in front of the other gave me the energy to take another step. I could feel my heart pounding, could hear it in my head. I gasped for breath, but there seemed to be an oxygen shortage. This was the most exhausting race I had ever run, and it was only a mile.

Heading into the final lap, an accusing voice inside said, *Look what you've done. You've ruined your body. And it's all your fault!*

I won the race, but my time was worse than the times I had run in ninth grade three years before. I also won the 2-mile that day, but for agonizing moments, I seriously doubted I would even be able to finish. Again my time was lousy. I slipped away as soon as possible after the meet to avoid any other officials who were certain to be making comparisons and would want to know, "What's wrong, Mary?"

Mary knew what was wrong. At least she hoped she did. She realized the weight she had regained wasn't muscle, not yet anyway. It would take a few more weeks to recondition herself.

Compounding her frustration with a subpar senior track season was the continued pressure to decide which college she would be attending in the fall. And when the University of Virginia informed Mary that the amount of aid they could offer would depend on her times during track season, she made her decision. She sent a letter of intent to Georgetown University, where she already had the firm offer of a scholarship that would pay her full college expenses, including books and travel.

With that decision behind her, Mary could devote all her emotional energies to running well again. She won Wilkes-Barre's annual Cherry Blossom Run for the fourth time. But the track times only slowly improved.

By May my times were approaching, though not surpassing,

the corresponding times from my sophomore year. My breathing still gave me some trouble, but other than that, running felt natural again. I couldn't help wondering how well I would be doing if I hadn't had to make up lost ground for more than half a season. But as the end of the season and the state championship loomed nearer, I began to regain my confidence.

One day in May I noticed a newspaper announcement for a TV movie entitled "The Best Little Girl in the World." The ad said it was the true story of a teenage girl suffering from an eating disorder known as *anorexia nervosa.* Since I didn't know much about it, I asked Mom to watch the movie with me.

I quickly recognized a number of parallels between the girl in the story and myself. The story began with the girl running. When her ballet teacher made an off-hand remark about weight one day, the girl began cutting down on her food intake and increasing her exercises. Her sit-up routine reminded me of my own—a hundred, morning and evening. Seeing her weigh herself every morning and study her body in the mirror reminded me of my own actions only months before.

Like me, she bickered with her dad at mealtime about the amount of food she was eating, and she had trouble concentrating in school. Watching her growing obsession with the idea of losing weight long after she passed her original goal brought the painful realization: *I was just that bad, that irrational, that obsessed!*

As the character in the story began to waste away until her physical and emotional health were broken, I cried. I looked around the den at the shelves Dad had made to display all my ribbons and medals and trophies. On the walls were framed photos of me—running, receiving awards. I thought about the four years of expensive college education that running was going to pay for. I looked again at the actress playing the pitiful girl on TV, and I confessed to my mother in between sobs, "To think, I almost ruined my life!"

Mom hugged me as I cried. I think she must have felt as relieved as I to finally have an explanation for what had happened to me during the winter. I had had anorexia. *Anorexia nervosa.* Just giving it a name answered so many questions that had plagued me.

"Everything's going to be all right, Mary," Mom reassured me.

"I know," I said. And I believed it. *It's over,* I told myself. *I'm eating again. Just like that girl in the story. And now that I know what to watch for, I'll never become anorexic again.*

"Everything is fine now, Mom."

But we were both wrong.

Chapter 10

What I didn't tell my mom—what I didn't tell anybody—was what was going on in my mind those last months of my senior year. During the winter of drastic dieting, I had been so hungry that thoughts of food haunted me.

If I ate a bowl of cereal before I left for school, that image would stay on my mind until lunch, to be replaced by the image of what I had eaten for lunch. I found it difficult to take notes in class. In the middle of conversations with friends in the hallway, I'd see food instead of faces. At first, the only relief from these images was my running. But before long, I began to notice that words would echo through my mind in tempo with the beat of my feet hitting the ground—*sand-wich, sand-wich, sand-wich, sand-wich.* The last thing I ate, whatever that happened to be, dogged my footsteps wherever I went.

Schoolwork that had always come easily for me now consumed unprecedented time and concentration. Late one warm spring evening, after spending far too long trying to decide on a subject for a poetry-writing assignment, I finally poured out my frustration in a poem: "The Struggle of a Poet":

> "Why do I make things so difficult?"
> Is the question I always ask.
> A chore that is simplistic
> Becomes a major task.

I'm moving at a snail's pace
While others seem to fly.
This project is taking hours
As the world passes by.

The poem, describing my feelings over the assignment itself, covered an entire page and spilled over onto the back.

My English teacher gave me an "A" for the poem. She said she liked the expression of emotion. I don't think she had any idea that the emotions went much deeper than the words I had scratched on that blue-lined notebook paper.

It is doubtful that anyone suspected the severity of the turmoil churning inside Mary. All her acting experience served her well as she laughed and smiled, going through the motions of the final month of her senior year. Bob came home from college to take her to the prom. And all the pre-graduation preparations went pretty much as planned.

By the end of the track season, she was even running well again. And after a fourth straight district championship in the 2-mile run, she went to the states, where she captured her second state championship. Though she was happy and relieved with her first-place finish, the victory prompted far less emotion than she had felt after the cross-country championship seven months earlier. Her times were still disappointing, matching only her best times during tenth grade. She wanted to prove she could do better.

Pleased and proud of their daughter's success and evident recovery, the Wazeters wrote a thank-you note to Coach Watkins, expressing their appreciation for his influence on Mary as an athlete and as a person. They thanked him for his years of coaching and for the concern and counsel that had not only resulted in Mary's victorious senior running seasons but also helped her survive what they called "Mary's recent near-anorexia."

Mary, like her parents, took her weight recovery, her improved and improving physical fitness, and her regular eating habits as evidence that she had beaten anorexia. What Mary didn't understand was her ongoing preoccupation with food.

Convinced that I hadn't reached my peak for the season, I decided to run one more race. So on May 30, one week after I took the state championship, I caught a bus to New York where I planned to enter the L'Eggs Minimarathon.

During the two-hour ride over the mountains and across New Jersey, I opened a *Seventeen* magazine and began to read what looked like an interesting article. When I got to the end, I realized I couldn't remember a thing the author had said. So I started over and reread every sentence. Twice. Three times. Still the meaning of the words didn't register. The only image in my mind was that of a packet of crackers in my purse.

I closed the magazine in frustration and tried to take in the spring-green hillsides outside the bus window. But no matter how the scenery changed, I still saw crackers.

Shrugging my shoulders, I gave in and fished out the cellophane package. Just after I broke the air-tight seal, I opened my magazine and began to read again. But the crunch of crackers in my mouth sounded as loud as a jackhammer to my ears, making concentration impossible. I closed the magazine, shut my eyes, and chewed.

When the crackers were gone, I crumpled the empty package and poked it into the ashtray in the arm of my seat. I picked up the magazine once more. This time I saw not only the packet of crackers, but heard their fresh crunchiness and tasted their saltiness.

What's wrong with me! I wondered. *I can't even read a magazine article.* Realizing I had only three months before college, I felt more frightened than frustrated. Something was terribly wrong with me and I couldn't imagine what.

My brother Gerry and his girlfriend, Sandy, met me at the station. And by the time they delivered me to the starting line in Central Park the next morning, I had pushed my new concern to the back of my mind and focused my attention on the biggest race I had ever entered.

Before the start, I was supposed to meet some friends from the Warren Street Social and Athletic Club, an amateur running group I had first learned about back in tenth grade. I had run with them in a few roadraces and planned to be part of their team in this one. But as we wound our way through the pre-race mêlée of five thousand women runners, I doubted I would be able to spot anyone I knew. My friends had said they'd be waiting under the biggest tree in front of the Tavern on the Green, and sure enough, they were there.

Tracy Sundlun, the highly respected coach of the Warren Street team, gave us our instructions, reminding us, "Don't start too fast. It's already ninety degrees and the heat's going to get worse. And, Mary," he added, singling me out, "since you don't know the course, just stick with one of the other Warren Street runners and follow the crowd."

Giant loudspeakers mounted on trucks called the runners to the start. The entire Warren Street team found a place near the front of the pack. Ahead of us, in the front row, were the top-ranked runners. The cameras were trained on them. And I could see Greta Waitz, probably the premier woman's distance runner in the world at that time, giving a last-minute interview.

I looked around at that massive crowd. There were far too many people to notice individual faces; what I saw looked like a sea of colorful running outfits amid thousands of stretching, shaking, moving arms and legs. My heart accelerated at the sight; I had never seen a race like this, let alone run in one.

The gun sounded and we were off. By the time I'd run the first mile and a half in the smoldering heat and the smoggy haze that hung over the park, most of the runners who had started like rabbits were now making like turtles. I passed more than a few who had given up altogether. With my natural endurance, I had always been a strong hot-weather runner. And I was in good shape from all the speed work I'd done during track season. So despite the heat, I was running comfortably.

The longer I ran, the more the conditions took their toll on the field. I kept passing runners but had no idea how many were still ahead of me. And I still felt good.

Into the third mile I was surprised to hear someone call out to me, "You're number twenty!" I had no idea I was running that well. I felt great.

I felt even better starting the fourth mile when someone reported, "You're number twelve!" I had obviously passed eight more; I'd lost count.

In the next two miles I caught and passed three more runners, and then one more. With a mile to go I pulled up closer to a woman I had been following much of the race. I concentrated on her back except for the fleeting moments when I looked up and saw the skyline looming ahead of us. With a half-mile to go, I finally caught her, matched her stride for stride, and then pulled slightly ahead—but not before I had recognized her as a runner whose career I had admired for some time. Surprised to find myself running with someone of her caliber, I tried to hold my position and kick for the finish.

The crowd lining the road for the last mile screamed like people possessed. The excitement kept my adrenaline pumping. But at the end she came sprinting past me and crossed the finish line two seconds ahead of me. Joan Benoit, future U.S. Olympic marathon champion, took seventh place and I settled very happily for eighth.

I had barely crossed the finish line before a bunch of the Warren Street guys swarmed me, literally jumping up and down in their excitement. The coach shouted, "Mary! Do you know what you just did? Do you know what you just did?" I knew I had run a good race, but I had never expected a reception like this.

The race officials informed me I needed to stay nearby for the awards ceremony, and newspaper reporters wanted to know who

I was and what I thought about the race. My brother Gerry finally found me to give me a celebratory hug. And as we waited near the finish for the rest of the field to come in, a number of shoe-company representatives introduced themselves. A man from Adidas asked me if I was running for anyone. I explained that I ran for another company, but admitted that I had always preferred Adidas. He took down my name and address, indicating he would get in touch to let me know what Adidas could do for me.

I also talked to a Nike rep. And since Nike furnished the shoes for the Georgetown cross-country program, he too promised to be in touch.

As the other Warren Street runners finished the race, they gathered around to congratulate me. And there was a steady stream of photographers and mini-cam crews asking me to pose. In the commotion I didn't even know who was taking photos for what.

Finally the race officially ended and the awards ceremony began. Greta Waitz, the first-place winner, gave a short victory speech and received her trophy. Then the rest of the top ten finishers were called up to the platform. I received a large silver bowl. As cameras clicked and motordrives whirred all around, I felt like pinching myself to see if I would wake up and discover the whole thing had been a dream. After all the failures, all the disappointments, this day was almost too wonderful to believe.

Indeed, finishing eighth in the L'Egg's Minimarathon catapulted Mary into the upper ranks of the running world. She beat out a number of world-class athletes and finished in impressive company. In addition to Greta Waitz and Joan Benoit, other award winners included Jacqueline Gereaux, a former winner of the Boston Marathon, and a couple of the best women runners from New Zealand.

So Mary went home to Wilkes-Barre, more excited about the incredible outcome of the L'Eggs race than concerned about the reading trouble she had had on the way to New York. In the blur of activity following this event, her eating problem took a back seat.

Everyone at school heard about the race. In every class someone would say, "Hey, Mary. Saw your picture in the *New York Times.*" Or "Mary, did you see the *Daily News?* You made page one!"

The school's annual year-end awards ceremony was scheduled for a couple days after I got back. At Meyers it was termed "Moving-Up Day," because the entire senior class took seats of honor on the stage of the auditorium, while the remaining classes moved up to take each preceding class's place.

I knew I would win the school's Scholar-Athlete Award, an honor that meant a lot to me because my brother David had won it three years before, and also because I still wanted to be known as a well-rounded person. So I wasn't surprised when my name was called; I hurried out to the front of the stage to accept the plaque and the applause of my fellow classmates.

I wasn't at all sure, though, about the other award I was secretly hoping to receive. The phys ed department always selected the winner of the Beatrice Rosenthal Award for outstanding senior female athlete. I wanted that award for several reasons: First, because the girls' running program was such a new sport at Meyers that no runner had ever won it, and my winning would help establish cross-country and track as a legitimate sport. There was a selfish motive too: I really wanted to see my name go up on the permanent plaque in the trophy case that stood in the front lobby of the school!

When the head of the phys ed department stepped to the microphone to announce, "The winner of the Beatrice Rosenthal Award for this year's top female athlete at Meyers High School goes to . . . ," my dancing heart did a stutter-step. And when the PA system echoed, "Mary Wazeter," I felt like sprinting down to the microphone. But I walked instead, savoring the applause of classmates and friends. And at that moment, the warm sounds of affirmation very nearly made up for the personal feelings of rejection I had experienced in the past four years. It was the high point of my life at Meyers High School.

But Mary didn't rest on her laurels. Her Warren Street friends had been so excited by her finish in the L'Eggs race that they urged her to come back to New York the next weekend to run in a 10-Kilometer race in New Jersey. "There won't be nearly as big a field just a week after the L'Eggs. And the way you've been running, you might walk away with it."

Mary had hesitated, recalling the Georgetown coach's instruction to take it easy during the summer. But she also knew that she hadn't yet reached her peak after a slow track season, and the taste of success had whetted her competitive appetite. So before she left New York, she agreed to take part in the competition.

At the end of the week, she headed for New York once again—this time in the family car, with her father driving. The Sumol 10K race was part of the annual Portuguese festival in Newark and was sponsored by a Portuguese soft-drink company. Race day was hot again and the course wound through cobblestone streets with an old-world feel before merging into the drab gray scenery of industrial Newark.

Mary finished first among the women. Her prize turned out to be one of her tallest trophies ever and first-class airfare to Portugal to run in an international race late in August.

But there was little time to relish this new victory. Mary returned home to a week crammed with graduation activities. There was practice for the ceremonies at school, graduation parties and receptions in the homes of friends, and a special dinner given in her honor by her folks.

As I sat and watched my blue-and-gold-robed classmates parade across the stage to receive their diplomas, my mind was whirling. *I made it,* I told myself. *I set myself the goal of a state championship and I made it. I set out to win the Scholar-Athlete*

Award and I made that. I even won the Rosenthal Award. And now in the past two weeks, I've come in eighth in the L'Eggs race against an international field and first in the Sumol 10K, with the chance to run in Portugal later in the summer. I've already made up for the poor showing during track season and everything is starting to fall into place. I'm running better now at 95 pounds, better than ever before. All the work, all the running, even the food problems have been worth it. And I'm still improving. Maybe I'll run one more race, maybe the Irish Heritage out at Harvey's Lake at the end of the month, just to see how I do.

Once graduation was over, with nothing to occupy Mary's mind but the daily routine and her training, thoughts of food returned in force. Bob came home from college and took her out a few times, but Mary couldn't bring herself to tell him about this strange obsession that drove every other thought from her brain except the smell, the feel, the taste of food in her mouth.

To Bob and her other friends, Mary seemed detached and disinterested. She talked about her hopes and plans for her next race, for Georgetown, even for the next Olympics. But what she conveyed to Bob was boredom with him and a deepening self-absorption. And his calls came fewer and farther between.

On one of our last dates, Bob and I went to a movie. I don't recall the name of it, but it must have been a comedy. I remember sitting in the theater and hearing people laugh all around me. I even remember hearing Bobby laugh. I thought, *What's so funny?* While everyone else was viewing a movie on the screen, I saw only my supper—replaying like a short loop of videotape—over and over in my mind.

My sister Judy came home for a visit in mid-June, and I hinted at my problem to her. "I don't know what's wrong with me," I said. "But I just can't get the images of food out of my mind."

Judy suggested that I pray more and meditate on some Bible

passages. I didn't tell her I couldn't even read, let alone meditate on Scripture. In an indirect way I even blamed God for my problem. *If he hadn't created food,* I muttered to myself, *I wouldn't have this craving.*

On June 20 I received a surprise phone call from Tracy Sundlun of the Warren Street Club. "If you can be in New York tonight, you've got an all-expense-paid trip to Aruba tomorrow. There's going to be a 10K race three days from now. Can you do it?"

I told Tracy I would have to check and call him back. When I explained the proposition to my parents, they agreed that this was too good an opportunity to pass up. While Dad and Judy packed my suitcase, I called my boss at Kistler Pool, where I served as a lifeguard for the summer, to arrange for someone to cover for me for the next few days.

Three hours after Tracy's call, I was on a bus again, heading for New York. The next morning I boarded a plane and took off on the first overseas flight of my life. A month before I had been hoping against hope that I would finally win my state championship in track. Now I was a big-time athlete, jetting off to compete in my first international roadrace. My life had suddenly moved into the fast lane, and I wondered if I could keep up.

The race sponsors provided the invited runners with rooms in the swankiest resort hotel on Aruba. I had never imagined, let alone seen anything so luxurious. Huge tropical plants decorated the inside and outside of the hotel. My private room had two beds, a sauna, and a balcony overlooking the ocean. I nearly choked the first time I saw the prices on the menu at the nicest of the three hotel restaurants. My hosts reassured me that I was to have whatever I wanted—all weekend. And that I was there at their expense.

But arriving two days before the race, I found too much time on my hands—or more specifically, on my mind. All around me was the beauty of a tropical island. Snow white beaches. Tall, stately coconut palms. An ocean that stretched in blue-green hues for as far as the eye could see. But I didn't see any of it. I only saw the same old scenery. Food.

I had packed a Bible in my suitcase. So I took it down to the beach and tried to follow Judy's advice. It didn't work. I sat on the sand, looking out over one of the most beautiful gems in the crown of creation, and a wave of lonely despair washed over me. *Not even God can help me. What am I going to do?*

So consumed was Mary with thoughts of food and hopelessness that she went through the pre-race preparations in a daze. She lost a pink sweater, misplaced a room key, and then had to explain how she had left one of the hotel's towels on the beach where she had been sunbathing. Her two Warren Street teammates laughed and chalked up Mary's absent-mindedness to youthful excitement and pre-race jitters. But what happened the morning of the race was not so laughable.

Somewhere a distant ringing summoned me to groggy consciousness. *The phone.* I rolled over in the morning light and lifted the receiver. "Mary, where have you been? Everyone is looking for you. You were supposed to be down at the starting line a half an hour ago." The voice was that of one of the Warren Street girls.

"I guess I overslept. What time is it?"

"Nearly a quarter to eight. The race starts in less than twenty minutes. You better get out here."

I dropped the phone and rolled out of bed. Five minutes later I yanked on my running suit, pulled on a pair of socks, tied my shoes, and raced out the front doors of the hotel. There wasn't another competitor or hotel vehicle in sight. And with the starting line of the race over a mile down the road, there was nothing to do but run.

I reached the starting line with less than ten minutes to spare—hardly enough time to catch my breath before the gun sounded and the entire field took off. I had already loosened up, so I started fast on what was the most unusual course I had ever run. The road headed inland through groves of palms and then into a countryside dotted with adobe huts. Laughing children ran out of the huts to watch as I ran by. Wild goats looked up from their grazing to see who or what was foolish enough to be running in the tropical morning heat.

I still held my lead as the course twisted back out to the shoreline where the sound of waves rolling onto the beach sounded louder than the spectators at many of my previous races. That last beautiful stretch of road seemed like something out of a travel agency ad.

I crossed the finish line well ahead of the second-place runner. But the thrill of victory was dampened by the realization that I had nearly missed the race altogether. Misplacing clothes and forgetting keys might be annoying and embarrassing. But forgetting to show up for a race I had flown 2100 miles to compete in would have been unforgivable. And I had come within ten minutes of doing just that!

Just when so many things in my life seemed to be falling into place, I was somehow losing control.

Chapter 11

I had intended to take a break from running after Aruba. But when I realized the Irish Heritage race—an annual local event—was only days away, I decided to enter. I hadn't forgotten the Georgetown coach's orders to take a break; I simply told myself, *You're already in shape. It's not as if you'll have to work hard. It's just one more race. Then you can take some time off.*

On June 27 I won the women's division of the Classic and took home one of my favorite prizes ever—a beautiful little shamrock pin with a diamond in the middle. With this victory, my third straight in roadraces, I decided to enter just one more race—the prestigious and very popular Pepsi 10K, scheduled over the Fourth of July weekend in New York City.

My trip to New York was the third since spring track season. Unlike the L'Eggs race, where I had only hoped for a good showing, this time I wanted to win. But the decision to run yet another race wasn't only a quest for another victory; anticipating and planning for the race, any race, gave my mind a rest from the addictive thoughts of food.

The morning of July 5 was clear and very hot. I had been running strong in summer heat, so I took the weather as a good omen. When I saw the crowd of more than four thousand runners congregating around the starting line in Ft. Lee, New Jersey, just across the river from Manhattan, I had to suppress some niggling doubts.

Fortunately, by virtue of my times in earlier races, I was assigned a good starting position. So when the starting gun sounded and the crowd began to surge out across the upper level of the George Washington Bridge, most of the stampeding herd was behind me.

Never in my racing career had I felt the emotions I experienced early in that race. As I took the gradual incline of that bridge high over the Hudson River, the scenic palisades stretched upriver as far as I could see. The massive steel structure of the bridge loomed overhead, while downriver to the south, the skyline of Manhattan jutted into the summer blue sky. Despite my plan to start conservatively in order to gauge the heat and the competition, the thrill of running in such a huge crowd and the visual splendor of the world's most glamorous city had me so hyped that I began the race with one of my fastest miles ever.

Though I wasn't absolutely sure, by the time we descended the bridge and began winding along the cordoned-off streets of New York City, it appeared I was already ahead of the rest of the women's field. But my jackrabbit start was also taking its toll. With each jarring footfall on blistering pavement, I could feel the strength ebbing out of my legs. And for every lungful of ninety-degree air I sucked in, I had to exhale another breath full of energy. As the heat sapped me from inside and out, I forced one leg to follow the other.

At the three-and-a-half-mile mark I headed up a hill that in my fatigue looked and felt Himalayan. I expected the field to catch up and spring past me any moment and I berated myself with every step. *Why did you have to start so fast? Why didn't you try to save something to fight this heat? Just keep going. Keep moving. Hang on. You gotta hang on.*

Only 35 minutes and 13.8 seconds after the start in New Jersey, I crossed the finish line in Manhattan's Inward Park. The second- and third-place women finishers came in a minute and a half behind me. I had won the biggest victory of my running career.

As rewarding as the victory was, I got just as big a kick out of the awards ceremony, where I shared the spotlight with the first-place men's winner, marathon champion Bill Rogers. I gave him a hug and kiss and we stood on the victory stand together, holding our trophy bowls aloft for the photographers.

I rode home the next day nearly overwhelmed by my good fortune. For years I had wanted to meet my long-time running idols, Bill Rogers and Greta Waitz. And now in the course of half a summer, I had stood with both of them and posed for victory photos.

Mary's feelings of accomplishment were bolstered by the affirmation of her friends, her family, and the media. The July 6 New York Times *carried a picture of the race and cited Mary along with Bill Rogers as the winners. On July 7 her hometown paper carried a story and picture under the headline, "Wazeter Now One of Best in Country." After years of struggling with her confidence as a runner, Mary was beginning to believe in her potential. For so long she had hoped to be good enough to win a college scholarship. Now, for the first time, she dared to dream of the Olympics.*

But the summer's growing stockpile of wonderful memories wasn't sufficient to crowd the obsessive food thoughts from Mary's mind. The more she realized her own lack of control over those thoughts, the more discipline she exerted over every other aspect of her life.

Almost every day of that summer, when I wasn't racing or traveling to a race, I followed the same routine. I was up soon after dawn to run five miles. Then I would walk the four blocks north on Old River Road to St. Theresa's Catholic Church for morning Mass, where I'd pray that those bothersome food thoughts would go away and leave me alone. Afterward I'd go home and eat a bowl of cereal for breakfast and try to ignore the image of that cereal in my mind as I headed across town to my job at Kistler Pool.

I often worked seven days a week to make up for the time I

took off for running. For the first couple of hours after the pool opened every morning, I would give swimming lessons to preschool or elementary-school kids. Then I worked as a lifeguard until my shift ended at seven o'clock in the evening.

I ran again when I got home, clocking at least ten miles for the day before allowing myself to eat supper. Bedtime proved the most troublesome part of my routine. For as long as I could remember, I had eaten a small snack before retiring for the night. But this summer, in an effort to exercise some control over food, I forced myself to retreat to my room without so much as a glass of milk.

Despite my good intentions, my body, or perhaps it was only my mind, refused to go to sleep without something in my stomach. I'd lie awake for hours, often until two or three o'clock in the morning. Sometimes I would turn on the light to read. Much of the time I tried to think about races and running to crowd out the image of cookies and milk or a picture of a bowl of ice cream. When I would finally fall into an exhausted sleep, I tossed restlessly and dreamed of food.

I tried as many strategies as I could think of to keep my mind off food while I worked. For one thing, I made my daily lunches deliberately unexciting. All summer long at the pool, I ate the same thing at the same time. At three o'clock sharp, I would take my break and walk over to the concession stand to order a hot dog with mustard, a banana, and a medium diet soft drink. I imagined that if I didn't have to think about what I would eat, if I made the decision once and for all, then I wouldn't be as likely to think about the food before it was mealtime. But it didn't work that way.

As the summer dragged on and my meal became more and more familiar, that hot dog, banana, and pop became a bigger and brighter picture in my mind. The hours dragged like days as I watched the hands on the big outdoor clock inch slowly, slowly toward three o'clock.

The most unpleasant part of my day was teaching the

morning swimming classes for the little kids. I had to get into the pool to teach, and the chill of the water absorbed every bit of the warmth from my body within seconds of the time I stepped in. Between the bone-chilling cold and the food flashing through my mind, I found it nearly impossible to concentrate on the business at hand.

I loved the kids who came for lessons—their excitement about the water and about learning. And the love and the trust I received from those kids should have given me real satisfaction. Instead, it inspired fear.

It was with great alarm one morning that I snapped out of a daze—I had been thinking about a bowl of cereal again—to find a half-dozen kids splashing all around my end of the pool. Two of them were dog paddling in water over their heads, and I had no idea how long they had been horsing around without my conscious supervision.

Mary, what's wrong with you, I accused myself. *You can't even fulfill your responsibilities when little kids' lives are at stake. How can you be so cruel and uncaring?* I hated myself for my irresponsibility.

Conversations with friends became potential minefields of embarrassment; I never knew when my mind would flip out on food and I'd lose the sense or the subject of what the other person was saying. Neither of us would realize I was gone until a question was asked or some awkward pause yanked me back to reality without a clue as to what I should say.

I tried to avoid idle chatter at the pool by taking books with me. Whenever I had a break, I'd go off to the side by myself, pretending to be engrossed in my reading, and trying to remember to turn the pages at a regular and realistic pace.

I remember only one book from the many I pretended to read—a biography of St. Theresa of Lisieux, a Carmelite nun who was also known as the "Little Flower Saint." I started reading the book because she was the saint for whom our local church was named. But I became intrigued by the accounts of her selfless disregard for food. She was so concerned about the needs of others that she gave away most of her food to those who needed it more than she. I couldn't help comparing my own selfishness and obsession with her witness of sacrifice. Her example challenged me and convinced me that I wasn't anything like that, and I hated my weakness as much as I admired her.

For a time, I hid what was going wrong inside me. My constant reading put off any friends who happened to be at the pool, and fear of the possibly tragic consequences helped me maintain my concentration with the little kids. But slip-ups did occur.

One day the director of the pool called to me during one of my breaks. He had a mop and a plunger in his hand. "I need you to come with me, Mary. One of the toilets in the women's bathroom is stopped up. I need you to stand guard outside while I'm in there fixing it."

"Okay."

He knocked on the ladies' room door. When he got no response, he instructed me, "Tell anyone who wants in that we should be back in service in just a couple minutes."

"Sure."

With nothing to do but wait, my mind quickly wandered to my upcoming hot dog. And the next thing I knew a middle-aged woman was hastily exiting the rest room, followed thirty seconds later by my red-faced boss. "Where were you, Mary?" he screamed furiously. "How did that lady get into the rest room?"

"I don't know," I mumbled. And it was the truth. I had no idea.

"You don't know? Where did you go?"

"Nowhere. I was right here. She must have just slipped by—"

"Slipped by? How could she slip . . . aaugh!" He shook his head and swore. "Guard the door, willya? I don't want any more surprise visitors, okay? I'll be done in two more minutes. Don't move. Don't even blink."

The second time I successfully stood my post. No one else

even came along before my boss came out again, still shaking his head and muttering under his breath.

As the summer rolled by, my frustration continued to mount. I couldn't sleep at night. I fretted all day about my lack of concentration. Only running gave me an emotional outlet. So I kept up my daily workouts, ignoring my conscience, which constantly reminded me that the Georgetown coach had ordered me to take a month off.

An official from the Wyoming Valley Striders, a local running club, called to ask me to participate in a discussion of roadracing at a panel to be held on the day before that group's big summer race, the seventh annual Wyoming Valley Striders 20-Kilometer Run. I hadn't been planning to run in the race, but I told the man I would be glad to be on the panel scheduled for July 19.

A few days before the race I saw a flyer promoting the race. It listed me among the name runners scheduled to compete and take part in a panel discussion. Over the next few days, I saw my name in the newspaper, on bulletin boards, in store windows—wherever the race was promoted.

"I don't really want to run tomorrow," I confessed to my friend Chuck who had run with me on the morning of July 19.

He shrugged. "Then don't."

"But I feel obligated. I told them I'd be on the panel. And they've used my name in all the pre-race publicity. I feel like I'll be letting them down if I don't run." What I didn't say was that I didn't want my local running friends to think I was too big now to run a local race.

"Mary," Chuck said. "Don't feel like you have to do this to please other people. Do what you want to do."

But I couldn't decide, and as I went to bed that night, I still hadn't come to a decision. *It's a simple decision. I'm either running or I'm not. Which will it be?*

Mental gymnastics kept me tossing and turning for hours. First I worried about the Georgetown coach finding out I had run still another race. Then I would think about the Striders, people I had known and run with for years in races near Wilkes-Barre; they were counting on me. Still, I needed a rest. . . . Yet I had been running so well all summer that I felt certain I could win. No, it was just a local race, and though there would be a number of excellent runners from throughout the northeast, it was still nowhere near as prestigious as the New York races. On the other hand, If I didn't run, I'd have to watch someone else win a race I knew I could have taken easily—

At three in the morning I was still debating. So I sat up, turned on the light, and tried to take my mind off the issue by reading a book until I couldn't keep my eyes open any longer. Even then, sleep wouldn't come. When the first rays of the morning sun finally cracked the sky, I was unrested . . . and still undecided.

Chapter 12

When my parents woke up that morning, I told them about my reluctance to run. They gave me the same advice Chuck had given me: "Don't run unless you feel like it."

To make the decision even harder, I was restless—the kind of restlessness that acted as a catalyst for my adrenaline and often signaled a good race. I *had* to run.

As in every other race that summer, the weather was sultry. And after a night of emotional tension, I ran easily at first, trying to work out all the tightness and uncertainty. Twelve miles was a long race, and I wanted to hold something in reserve against the heat.

But I kept the lead woman runner in sight at all times as we headed north out of Kirby Park and along the river. With each mile I felt stronger and looser, and each mile I ran a little faster than the mile before. I passed the leading woman long before we reached the halfway mark. And as the race wore on, I found myself passing men I recognized, good local runners who usually finished ahead of me in roadraces. Either the heat was taking a severe toll or I was running a very strong race—or both.

I crossed the finish line more than six minutes ahead of the old course record for women. The men's winner, a former U.S. Olympian, and I took home huge silver cups, and once again I made a splash in the local newspapers.

A few days later, Mary got the official word: her time of 1:15:26 was a national record for women in her age group. A week after the post-race headlines, one of the Wilkes-Barre papers featured Mary with a big write-up and picture on the sports page. The article recounted her successes, told of her plans to run in Portugal at the end of the summer and for Georgetown in the fall. In the article, Mary gave no hint of her private pain. The photo, showing her in running garb and a toothy grin, was captioned: "Mary Wazeter and Winning Smile." And the article ended this way:

> Because she is working eight hours a day at Kistler Pool, she isn't training this month. However, next month she plans to run 10 miles a day.
>
> Despite all the recent publicity, the runner, who always sports a pleasant smile, doesn't worry about the outside pressure.
>
> "I take each day at a time. I try not to think about running all the time. I've had good times and some bad times and I've learned from both."
>
> Whatever the times, Wazeter's running is taking her distances that most people only dream about.

They weren't really lies—the one about not being in training when I had been running ten miles a day all summer, or the one about not feeling outside pressure; I just wasn't ready to face the truth.

But I couldn't escape the truth either. I would lie awake at night, thinking of food. And when sleepless nights became the norm, I would lie awake and worry about not sleeping. I did ease up on the running for a few days, but since running still provided my only effective emotional outlet, I soon increased the distance of my workouts again.

Lack of sleep began taking its toll in the days after my 20K victory. By the time I reached work each morning, I was dragging. I made it through the lessons by standing in the water with the kids. But once I got comfortable in my lifeguard chair, it was more than I could do to keep my eyes propped open. A couple times I was reprimanded for dozing on duty.

One afternoon I drifted off when some junior-high boys startled me awake. "Lifeguard! I'm drowning! I'm drowning!" I jerked myself to attention, jumped to my feet, and poised to take a dive before I heard the laughter and realized everyone in the pool was enjoying a joke at my expense. Everyone, that is, except the manager who called me in afterward for what could have been a stern lecture. Instead of being angry though, he expressed concern. I told him I hadn't been getting enough sleep and promised it would never happen again.

And as if my drowsiness didn't make me feel self-conscious enough, my physical exhaustion continued to affect my body's internal thermostat. The pool felt like the Antarctic Ocean as I taught my classes; my lips turned blue, my teeth chattered. Even sitting in the lifeguard chair under the blazing August sun, I could never seem to get warm enough.

Early in August, the race in Portugal was canceled. But the promoters promised to reschedule the trip sometime later. Though I had anticipated the trip all summer, I didn't feel disappointed. The start of college now became my primary focus. And step one in my initiation was another roadrace—Falmouth, Massachusetts, to be held late in August—the first race I would run in a Georgetown uniform.

Pan Fanaritis, the Georgetown coach, picked me up in a university car two days before the race. From Wilkes-Barre we drove to Long Island to spend the night with the family of the team's number-one runner, Pia Palladino. The ride gave me time for my first extended conversation with Pan, and we both used those hours on the road to learn more about each other. I asked a lot of questions about the team and about school. And Pan was more than happy to fill me in on my teammates and all the training routines. By the time we reached Long Island, I was more excited than ever about choosing Georgetown.

One look at the Palladinos' house as we pulled up into their driveway gave me some serious second thoughts. *Maybe I'm not going to fit into a school like Georgetown. Maybe my middle-class roots haven't prepared me for this.*

Pia and her family graciously attempted to set me at ease. As the evening progressed, everyone made a point to ask me questions about my family and my high school. I knew they were trying to be friendly, but the attention made me feel very much like the new kid on the block. And I didn't like the feeling.

Actually, Pia was one of the main reasons I had decided to go to Georgetown. She had a national reputation and I wanted someone like her on the team—someone I could learn from and who would present a challenge in every practice. Pan had told me that Pia was an excellent student, fluent in several languages. But when conversation turned to her summer experience on an archeological expedition in France, I felt incredibly unsophisticated. As much as the others tried to include me, I just didn't fit.

When I packed for the trip, I had included a stack of books I thought would impress everyone with my intellectual prowess. The books were just a front, of course, and even if they did make an impression, they only reminded me of my continuing struggle with concentration. I knew I would feel like an outsider until I could prove myself. And Falmouth would offer me the chance.

Another member of the Georgetown team joined us at Pia's for the drive up the coast. The three of us would run as a team. We drove the course of the race that afternoon and then on to the home of Chris Mullins's parents, where we would spend the night. Chris was a former Georgetown track star who had run in the Olympic trials and now competed in meets around the world. She and her fiancé, an Olympic steeplechaser, were also going to run in the race.

The Mullinses lived in an even more impressive home than the Palladinos. The decor looked like something out of *Better Homes and Gardens.* Once more I wondered, *Do I really belong here?* Since I was the only newcomer, I was again the focus of much polite, let's-get-to-know-you conversation.

Since I realized I would be sharing a major part of my life

over the next few years with some of these people—my two teammates and my coach—I did want to get to know them. And more than that, I wanted them to like me. I determined the first step in my personal win-friends-and-influence-people campaign would be a strong showing the next day in the Falmouth race.

Pia and I shared a room and a double bed that night. We gabbed for a while before going to sleep. She talked about her own adjustment to college life the year before and offered advice on what to bring to school. I asked a lot of questions about life on the Georgetown campus and about the team. I liked Pia, and she seemed to take a genuine interest in me. I hoped we could become friends.

After we turned out the light, I lay in the darkness and thought. About the new people I'd met. About school. About the race. About food.

I couldn't sleep.

Around midnight, sometime after Pia had dropped off to sleep, I slipped quietly out of bed, pulled on my robe, and went down the hall to Mr. and Mrs. Mullins's room. A sliver of light shone from under the door, so I knocked.

"Yes, what is it?" my hostess asked.

"Mrs. Mullins, it's Mary."

"What is it, dear?"

"I'm sorry to bother you, but I can't seem to get to sleep. Do you mind if I go down to the kitchen and fix myself a little something to eat?"

"Go right ahead, honey. Help yourself."

I tiptoed through the darkened hall, down the stairs and into the kitchen. When I opened the refrigerator, I saw just what I wanted—a nice big slice of apple pie.

I poured myself a glass of cold milk and had just sat down at the kitchen table when the back door opened and Chris's teenage sister, whom I had met earlier in the evening, walked in. Seeing her surprise at finding a house guest eating pie alone in her home in the middle of the night, I quickly explained: "I couldn't sleep and your mom said I could come down and get something to eat."

A few minutes later I was back in bed. But I still couldn't sleep. Instead, my mind focused on the very clear image of a big slice of apple pie—flaky light crust covering tart juicy apples. And no matter how hard I tried, I couldn't turn off the picture—not even by concentrating on the upcoming race.

From time to time I would lift my head and look at the digital clock beside the bed. 1:03. 1:38. 2:13. We had to be up at 5:30 to dress, eat, and drive to Falmouth. So as the night sped on at an alarming rate, I began to count down the time remaining to get some sleep. Three hours. Two hours. *Why can't I sleep? I've got to get some rest if I'm going to run well.*

Finally, I slid out from under the covers again and made my way to the bathroom. After gently closing the door, I flicked on the light and looked in the mirror. My eyes looked red and tired, my face drawn.

Glancing around the bathroom, I noticed a stack of reading material. So there in the early morning hours, surrounded by roomsful of sleeping strangers, with only the night sounds of a strange house for company, I sat atop the toilet lid and tried to read a copy of *The Preppie Handbook,* which a friend had given me as a joke. It didn't seem very funny.

By about five, my eyes seemed to grow almost irresistibly heavy. I turned off the bathroom light and crept back into the room with Pia and quickly fell asleep. When the alarm sounded a half hour later, I felt wretched.

At breakfast, when Pan asked how I was, I told him the truth. "I feel terrible," I said. "I didn't sleep all night."

"I'm sure you'll be all right, Mary." He obviously meant to be encouraging. "It's probably just a case of pre-race jitters. Once the race starts you'll feel fine." With that he seemed to shrug off the entire matter.

What he didn't know was that with a pattern of sleepless nights over the past few weeks, I had almost no physical reserves left. I wasn't all right. And I didn't think that would change at the sound of the starter's gun.

By virtue of my races earlier in the summer, I was one of the favorites. The field started fast. I started slow. But this time I wasn't conserving strength. I just didn't have any. Much of the course wound along the seashore, between the ocean on one side and gorgeous nineteenth-century mansions with park-like lawns and long Victorian porches on the other. When we had driven the course the day before, I had thought it was as beautiful as any I had ever run. But now I plodded along without so much as a glance at the palatial homes or the majestic shoreline.

Pan had instructed me to stick close to Pia. But after only two miles, exhaustion overcame me, and my entire body rebelled. My legs turned to lead. People passed me as if I were standing still, which was literally true a couple times when I had to throw up.

The only thing that kept me going was the humiliation I knew I would feel if I quit my first Georgetown race. Even so, I wasn't sure I could finish as I dragged myself up a long hill to the finish line.

I wanted to hide in the crowd at the end of the race. But Pan and Pia were there to congratulate me on my finish. I felt both sick and embarrassed, but they were both trying to tell me I had done well for what was merely a trial run before we began serious training for cross-country.

I knew, however, that I could have run much better if I had only gotten a few hours of sleep. I wanted to scream, "You don't understand! I'm better than this! Lots better!"

But I didn't say anything. Instead, I vowed to prove myself at the next opportunity.

Later that evening, back at the Mullinses' house, I overheard Mr. and Mrs. Mullins in the next room talking—about me. "Mary certainly is a nice girl," Mrs. Mullins was saying, "but something's troubling her."

If it's that obvious to people I met only yesterday, I mused, *I must be in worse shape than I thought.*

Chapter 13

I rode back to New York with Pan and took a bus home. By the time I reached Wilkes-Barre, I knew what I had to do. If I could no longer hide my problem, I would have to face it. And I would need all the help I could get.

I didn't reach home until early evening. Mom and Dad had read the race results that morning in the *New York Times.* So I didn't have to say much about that.

As soon as we walked in the door, I wandered into the kitchen with Mom. Dad took a seat at the dining room table in front of a mound of papers.

"Have you had anything to eat, Mary?" Mom wanted to know.

"Not since New York."

"I'll have supper soon. You must be hungry."

Now was the time. "I don't know whether I'm hungry or not."

"What do you mean, Mary?"

"Come in here, Mom," I said, ducking into the dining room. I looked from my dad sitting at the table to Mom standing in the doorway. Then I took a deep breath and began my confession. "I think there's something wrong with me."

Mom asked, "What do you mean, dear?"

"Well . . ." I tried to decide where to begin. "For one thing, I can't sleep at night. I lie in bed for hours and can't think of anything but food."

Dad frowned. "Do you feel guilty about eating, Mary?"

"I don't think so. But whenever I do eat anything, I see an image of that particular food in my mind. It's like a picture of the food—a slide—is projected into my brain. And I can't turn off the picture until I eat something else, and then there's a new picture.

"Sometimes when I'm running, the picture will fade out, and I'll hear voices naming the food. I'm never sure if I'm really hungry or just obsessed with food. I feel the same craving all the time."

I could see a cloud of concern settle over my parents' faces; I felt sure they were trying not to react with too much alarm as I continued.

"But what bothers me most is that I'm going off to college in a week and a half . . . and I can't read."

"You can't read?" Dad looked puzzled.

"When I try to read, my eyes see the words on the page, but all my mind sees is food. The words, the sentences don't make sense. I can't concentrate enough to make sense of one page, let alone all the material I'll have to read for college."

"How long has this been going on, Mary?" Dad asked.

"Pretty much all summer."

I could see that my answer upset Mom. "Mary," she exclaimed, "why didn't you say something sooner?"

"I don't know," I said. Now that I had opened up, I really didn't know why I hadn't said something long before now. "I guess I thought the problem would get better. But it only seems to be getting worse."

"I think we ought to get you in to see the doctor right away," Mom said. "We've got a routine physical scheduled before you leave for school anyway; I'll just call first thing in the morning and see if we can get in sometime tomorrow."

I went to see our family doctor the next afternoon with mixed emotions. It seemed good to finally be taking some step to get to the bottom of the problem. But I wasn't sure how I would handle it if there was something physically wrong. And if they didn't find anything—that would be just as discouraging. Maybe worse. At least most physical problems were treatable.

Mom sat with me in the examination room while the doctor gave me my physical. So she was there with me to hear his summary of the results: "We'll get all the forms filled out for Georgetown right away, Mary. You're in excellent physical shape. And I'm glad to see your weight is back up to 95 pounds." He was the doctor I'd seen back in the winter when I had dropped to an anorexic 89 pounds. He obviously felt I had made a complete recovery.

"There's just one problem, Doctor."

"Yes?"

I told him about my unusual preoccupation with food, and he stroked his chin and listened intently. When I finished he smiled, shrugged, and said, "Sounds to me like a clear case of pre-college jitters."

"But I think about food all the time. I can't read, I can't sleep, and—"

"You know, Mary," he said, "before my son went off to college he was so nervous he made himself ill. But once school started he got along just fine."

"But the thoughts don't—"

"Part of the problem may be that you're trying too hard not to think about the food. It's like telling yourself, 'I won't think about a pink elephant, I won't think about a pink elephant.' You're trying so hard not to think about it, you can't get it out of your mind.

"Why don't you try this? Next time you have a thought like that, don't try to repress it. Don't be afraid of it. Instead, think of the thought as your little friend."

The suggestion struck me as so absurd that I laughed out loud, more out of frustration than out of amusement. The doctor probably thought he had cheered me up with his insightful suggestion. He hadn't. I walked out of his office thinking, *He doesn't understand at all.* Whatever the problem, I knew it was more than a case of "pre-college jitters."

In the days that followed, the symptoms continued and Mary repeatedly expressed her concern to her parents. Despite her uncertainty about making the adjustment to college without resolving her problems, Mary wasn't ready to consider giving up the scholarship she had worked so many years to win.

She was frightened, but she was also determined to go on with her plans. Mary's parents talked to the coach about the problem, and the three of them tried to assure her that if the problem didn't correct itself, a counselor could be found at Georgetown to help her get to the bottom of it. The Wazeters also gave the coach a complete rundown on what had appeared to be anorexia; he told them he would keep a close eye on her and promised not to let her run if her weight dropped below 95 pounds.

So preparations continued. Mary and her mom assembled her fall wardrobe and started to pack for her first semester of college. Friends whose terms began before Georgetown's stopped in to say good-by. Some brought going-away gifts. And Mary's excitement and anticipation began to build.

Only a week before I was to leave for school, one of my closest friends, Kim Elinsky, invited me to go with her to the Jersey shore, where her parents had rented a hotel suite. Although it was the last weekend before school, my folks encouraged me to go, believing the change would be good for me after my long, hard summer.

Kim wanted to hit the beach the minute we arrived in Atlantic City. So while she went swimming, I lay in the sun on a beach towel, pretending to read. She finally coaxed me down to the water's edge, but the water felt so cold I refused to go in. That night we ate dinner in a restaurant with her parents, and I cleaned my plate. Afterward, shopping on the boardwalk, I bought a pound of fudge to take home to my folks.

Late that night, after everyone else in the suite was asleep, I slipped out of bed and went to the kitchen to raid the refrigerator. I spotted my box of fudge on the counter and ate a piece. Then another. And another. The next thing I knew I was sitting in a darkened kitchen with an empty fudge box; I had eaten the whole pound. I carefully buried the evidence deep in the bottom of the wastebasket and tiptoed back to bed and a night of restless tossing and turning.

I rose early and went out for a long, lonely run down the beach—three miles down and back along the almost deserted sand. But not even the sun rising over the rim of the sea could brighten the darkness I felt inside. I stopped once to stare out over the expanse of water, and its vastness made me feel so small and alone. I felt as if an ocean of misunderstanding stretched between me and my family, between me and anyone else who cared.

Later that day I worked up the courage to send out a distress signal; I confessed to Kim and her mom that I hadn't been able to read with comprehension and that I was worried, now that I was about to begin college. But they didn't understand either.

"You'll do great, Mary," Kim said. "You've always done so well in school. I'm sure there's nothing to worry about."

"Just relax, and I'm sure you'll do fine," her mom added. "And quit worrying about being number one."

"I wish I could," I replied.

I remained marooned. And my hopes for rescue dimmed a little more.

The next day Kim and I headed home together. About halfway, she stopped for ice cream. I succumbed to temptation and bought myself a double dip. But no sooner had we finished our treats and hit the road again than the guilt hit me. First the fudge, now the ice cream, not to mention the restaurant meals with Kim's folks. To make matters worse, I had a dinner date scheduled that same evening with a running friend from high school.

When Kim dropped me off, the first thing I did after greeting my folks was to run upstairs to the bathroom and step on the scales. My fears were confirmed. My weight had climbed to 96. *Before I go to Georgetown, I've got to drop a pound,* I vowed.

A couple days later my parents and I loaded all my things into the car and headed south for Washington, D.C. Somewhere along the way, I voiced my continuing uncertain feelings about the academic competition I knew lay ahead. "I don't really know if I should be doing this."

"Mary," my dad began, "at a school like Georgetown you're going to run into a lot of rich kids who've been around the world and had a few experiences you've never had. But you've done some things they've never done either. You've already proven yourself. Don't worry about the competition; you'll do fine."

But even after her parents unloaded her things and helped her get her dorm room organized, Mary told them good-by with no real sense of confidence that she was going to make it. And soon her sister Judy, who lived just across the river in Virginia, also had reason to doubt.

Judy came to visit Mary her first day on campus. They went together to take the orientation tour of the university library. Despite the clearly marked path, Mary kept getting turned around. When they finished, Mary surprised her sister by confessing she didn't think she'd understood anything they had just seen.

"It's just a library, Mary. You'll find your way around in no time," Judy assured her. But privately she thought Mary was acting strange, spacy, in a way she had never seen her before. And Judy vowed to herself to keep close tabs on her sister as the semester got underway.

There were other clues that Mary wasn't herself. Orientation included placement tests for some freshman subjects. She performed so poorly on the English and Spanish exams that she was placed in the lowest class in both subjects. Her coach questioned the results, however, and on the basis of her high-school record (English honors and four years of straight A's in Spanish), Mary was exempted from English Comp and placed in English Lit. The coach also saw that she was placed in a second-year Spanish class. Her other three classes—Theology, Philosophy, and American History—were already set.

By the time I'd been on campus for two days, I was increasingly aware that I might not be able to cope. One of the reasons I'd selected Georgetown was because of its small, compact campus. Now it seemed as big and sprawling and complex as some of the larger universities I'd visited.

I took my computer printout class schedule to the bookstore to get the texts I'd need. A sign right inside the door explained how to read the course number on my schedule and then where to find the corresponding coded books for the course. I read the sign three times before I gave up and simply began wandering up and down the aisles, looking from my schedule to the numbers on the shelves. Nothing made sense. A half-hour later I left the bookstore totally frustrated and headed straight for my coach's office. In tears I told Pan, "I can't find any of my books. I'm so confused."

He calmed me down with the promise to send someone else on the team over to help me decipher the bookstore system. But while I soon picked up all my books, the experience did nothing to bolster my confidence or my sense of independence.

None of the instructions we received in orientation seemed clear to me. For example, we were assigned to faculty advisors on the basis of our student I.D. numbers. When they announced the room location where my advisor would be, I made a note and arrived early enough to find a seat next to an extremely tall black student.

"Hi," I said. "I'm Mary Wazeter."

He nodded. "My name's Patrick Ewing."

"Oh," I said. "You're the basketball player. That explains

those photographers I saw following you around. I heard you were coming to Georgetown."

"Where you from?" he asked.

"Wilkes-Barre, Pennsylvania," I said, adding, "I'm a runner on the cross-country team."

But that's about as far as our conversation got before the advisor walked in and began to read the list of names on his roll. When he finished, he said, "Is there anyone here whose name I didn't call?"

I raised my hand. "You didn't call my name."

"Name please?"

"Mary Wazeter."

"You're not on my list. What's your I.D. number?"

I told him.

"You're in the wrong room, honey," he said. He gave me the room number where I was supposed to be, but by the time I got there, my advisor had dismissed his advisees and I had to make a special appointment to see him. Nothing seemed to be going smoothly.

On the first day of classes, my Spanish instructor gave all the instructions and assignments for the class in Spanish. Despite my four years of high-school Spanish, I could follow almost nothing she said. My philosophy professor may as well have been speaking a foreign language. And every one of my classes had a syllabus with a reading list a mile long. So I went straight to Pan and got his okay to carry only twelve hours instead of fifteen. Then I dropped American History and talked him into letting me into Spanish 101 instead of second year.

Mary knew immediately she wasn't going to be able to function without some kind of help. The daily routine proved to be a difficult challenge. Time and again she lost her way on the two-block walk from her dorm to the language lab, sometimes having to stop and ask directions two or three times. And when she got to the lab, she couldn't figure out how to run the tapes. A lab assistant helped her the first day, but in the days that followed she was too embarrassed to ask again. So she'd sit in the lab with the headphones over her ears, pretending to do her language study.

She was repeatedly late for philosophy class. The hallways of the science building where the class met all looked the same, and Mary often became disoriented. The fact that philosophy was her first class after lunch when thoughts of food were the most vivid and distracting didn't help either.

But finding the right classroom was no problem at all compared with the trouble she had following the course material. She listened in class, she even took notes. But nothing seemed to click.

Mary realized enough to know that something was terribly wrong, but all she would tell her coach was that she couldn't seem to keep up in class. He helped her find a student in each of her classes to go over assignments and study with her.

I wanted so desperately to make it. Again and again I'd ask my tutors to go over what I knew was the most basic material. I wanted to say to them, "I'm really not like this. Something is wrong with me." I wanted so much to succeed. But I knew they were thinking, "Mary is really dense." I felt so dumb.

I began to skip lunch on a regular basis, sometimes so I could have time to find my philosophy class. At other times I'd show up at the cafeteria and be turned away at the door because I'd left my ID card in the room. Occasionally I just didn't eat because I couldn't face the dizzying round of food thoughts that persisted after every meal.

The only thing I seemed to have under control was my running. I knew several members of the team already, and I felt accepted. The coach acted pleased with my times and didn't even seem concerned when I showed up for practice late a couple times the first week. He'd just say, "The team left ten minutes ago, but you can probably catch them if you take off now." Still, much of the time, I ended up working out pretty much on my own.

By the second week I was less certain than ever that I could make it in college. My sister Judy called every morning to make sure I was up and getting ready for class; and she'd pray for me over the phone. But every day I fell further and further behind.

My second week in college I called home every night in tears. "I can't take it," I'd tell my parents. "You're going to have to come and get me."

Dad would try to be positive. "There's no point in coming home, Mary. School has already started here. Pan says you're not doing that badly. He'll get whatever help you need—tutors, or whatever. Just hang in there."

But I'd cry and say there wasn't any help. I wanted to go home.

My parents would agree to leave first thing in the morning. I'd finally hang up. Then ten minutes later I'd call them back. "Don't come. I'll be all right. Let's give it a little time."

But deep down, I knew I needed more than time.

Chapter 14

I wasn't at all reluctant to ask for help—partly because I wanted people to know I thought something was wrong; I certainly didn't want them thinking I'd always been this way. My roommate saw my erratic behavior. She heard my flip-flop phone calls home. But she was a freshman, too, away from home for the first time and probably homesick; she had no idea how to help me.

Time after time I told the coach, "This isn't working. I don't know if I can make it here." He tried to help, arranged for tutors, tried to make it easy on me by not being too rigid or harsh, and kept insisting, "Everything's going to be fine." He was a laid-back optimist by nature and just didn't seem to understand the depths of my problem or of my growing despair.

Still, I kept proclaiming my need for help. To Judy. To my folks when we talked on the phone. I even went to the resident assistant in the dorm to say I was thinking of dropping out because I just didn't seem to be able to handle all the demands of college life. She told me, "One of the most common problems new students face is organization. What you need to do is get yourself on a schedule. Write down everything you need to accomplish during the day, and when it needs to be done. You'll feel a lot more in control."

I figured anything was worth a try. And I did feel better for the first couple days when I got up and made out a schedule; at least, I had a reassuring sense of where I needed to be, and when. But reviewing the schedule at the end of each day was a harsh self-indictment, damning evidence of my continuing failure.

Little things constantly screwed up my best-laid plans. Halfway across campus on my way to a class, I'd remember I had left my textbook in the room; by the time I returned to get it and finally reached class, the professor would be ending his lecture. I'd rush to the cafeteria for supper only to discover I'd left my ID and my keys in my locked dorm room with no idea of where to find my roommate. Then there was the day I missed every meal because I couldn't find my ID at all; the next day's schedule had to be completely rearranged, so I had to go to Student Affairs and complete a complicated replacement procedure.

Even when I did cross off some of the scheduled items on my "to do" list, I knew I'd only been going through the motions. One night, right after supper, when my agenda said: "Study Spanish in room," I sat across our shared desk from my roommate and just stared at my Spanish text. But nothing soaked in.

After a few minutes she stood up, stepped over to our little refrigerator and returned with an apple. When she took her first bite, the sound seemed to reverberate around the room at the decibel level of a rock concert. The amplifiers cranked up another notch with each subsequent bite.

I quickly gave up hope of concentration there and retreated to the dorm lounge in search of peace and quiet. But not even a TV blasting full volume could drown out the rustling of candy bar wrappers and the constant munching of hungry students. There seemed to be no place to study where I could escape the sight or sound of food.

Except the library. The signs inside the door say "No Food or Drinks." That thought sent me scurrying across campus. Once in the library I quickly found an empty table, pulled out my Spanish book, opened it to the assigned chapter, and stared at the vocabulary list. Sometime later, I realized I hadn't turned the page.

I glanced furtively around the room. No one seemed to notice. As I surveyed the students around me, I saw a girl who seemed intent on her book, stopping only occasionally to underline something. So I picked up my pen and searched the first page of my chapter for something to underline. Within minutes I had a well-marked page, but no idea of what it said.

Looking around again, I noticed a studious boy scribbling notes from his book onto an index card. When he finished, he placed the card on top of an inch-high pile of cards and pulled another blank one from his shirt pocket. So I pulled a cellophane-wrapped stack of cards out of my backpack and began taking my own notes. But nothing I wrote on those cards registered in my mind.

Finally, sometime between 1:00 and 2:00 A.M., I headed back to my room. My roommate was already sound asleep as I pulled out my schedule, crossed through the words "Study Spanish," and went to bed.

Every day I walked around campus, feeling invisible, an unseen observer who could watch but not really touch anyone else. Other people laughed and joked with each other. They moved purposefully from one building to another. They seemed so alive that I almost wondered if I was.

Within days after arriving at Georgetown, I'd begun to receive cards and letters from various friends at other colleges. Their obvious excitement about their new venture only heightened my despair. Bob sent me a birthday card and included a note: "Hi Mar, I know things are always hectic at first. Guess you're getting all settled in now though."

When I finished reading his card, I wondered what Bob and my other friends from home would think if they knew the truth. But the horror of that thought further depressed me.

During Mary's second week in school the cross-country team ran its first meet of the season, an eight-team invitational at James Madison. Mary forgot to eat breakfast the morning of the race and almost missed the team bus. In her rush she didn't even take her race shoes, just her practice pair. She felt sluggish and weak through the entire race. And a number of runners who ran away from her were some she'd beaten in high school or roadraces. So although she finished respectably in twentieth place, Mary shrugged off the congratulations of her teammates, knowing she should have done better.

Mary continued to talk to her parents every night. And when it became obvious things weren't getting better, the Wazeters drove down to Washington to talk to Mary's coach and set up some counseling appointments with a psychologist recommended by the school.

I was relieved that something was finally going to be done. I hoped the psychologist could help me. And when we met for the first time, I honestly confessed my frustrations with school. I told her about my study problems and my inability to cope with all the demands of college life. I wanted answers; I needed answers.

She listened for a while, asked a few questions to clarify points she didn't understand, and then she said, "I suggest one of the first things you try to do is keep a written schedule."

I couldn't believe I was hearing her right. I'd expected a lot more from a professional psychologist. I'd gotten the same advice from my RA and I already knew it wouldn't work. Some help counseling was going to be!

But I kept going back, twice a week, to meet for an hour with this lady who always served me tea and cookies. I talked, she listened. But I didn't think the counseling was doing a bit of good.

In fact, I seemed to be getting progressively worse. I kept losing things: I'd leave a pile of books in one of my classes and not remember until the room was locked up for the night; I lost another ID and had to go through the replacement rigamarole yet another time; three times I lost my dorm room key. I'd go down to the laundry room on the bottom floor of the dorm and put in a load of clothes. When I'd remember them two or three days later, I'd run down there to find some of them piled in the corner; the rest would have disappeared.

I felt sure my roommate and my teammates must have been talking about me behind my back. I knew I was acting spaced-out.

But while losing things frustrated me and embarrassed me, what troubled me even more was getting lost myself. I often became disoriented as I walked around the campus; but there were always people to ask for directions. There, I felt safe, sheltered.

Off campus was a different story.

One afternoon I arrived late for cross-country practice long after everyone else had started. So I decided to run by myself over near the Capitol and back, a meandering route I'd run a couple times with teammates. I zigzagged down the steep streets of Georgetown to the Potomac and along the river into Washington. I passed the Kennedy Center and headed up the mall past the Lincoln Monument. By the time I stopped for a breather at the Washington Monument, the sky was growing dark, and I felt the first drops of rain from some threatening clouds overhead.

I looked around. The streets seemed nearly deserted. *I know there's got to be a shorter way back to campus,* I told myself. And I looked for someone to ask directions.

Spotting a cluster of people bustling across the mall, I ran over. "Can anyone tell me the direction to Georgetown University?"

Of all the luck! They were French tourists who could barely make out my question, much less give me the answer. So I ran toward the White House, thinking that was the general direction and hoping I'd meet someone on the sidewalk who'd tell me the way. Suddenly the sky opened and rain fell by the bucketful; by the time I got to the ellipses on the south side of the White House, there was not a pedestrian in sight.

I kept running. When I spotted a man under an umbrella crossing the street at the next corner, I accelerated and caught up with him. "Excuse me, sir. Could you tell me the way to Georgetown University?"

"No, solly." When he turned around and smiled, I found myself facing a Japanese tourist.

Seeing no one else to ask and afraid to try some unknown route, I decided to retrace my steps. So I headed toward Foggy Bottom and the river, running along streets parallel to the national mall. Somehow in the darkness I made a wrong turn and went under a bridge I should have gone over. And when I finally found myself back at the Kennedy Center, I was on the opposite side of a six-lane expressway from where I thought I should be.

The rain was falling in sheets. The roads were clogged with rush hour traffic and I still didn't know how to get back. *It's dark. No one even knows where I am. It's cold. I'm going to catch pneumonia. Where am I?*

I could feel the panic creeping into my throat. *I have to get across that expressway.* With that thought and only that thought riveted in my mind, I scrambled and clawed my way up a wet, muddy embankment, climbed over the guardrail and sprinted across the first three lanes of traffic. There I had to pull myself up and over a concrete median barrier and watch for an opening in traffic. When it came, I raced across, jumped that guardrail and slid my way down another embankment to a street below.

Squinting into the rain, I could barely see the street sign at the next corner. But I knew where I was. And with a sigh of relief, I began to run toward campus. Two hours after the time I'd left, I walked into my room vowing never again to run by myself unless I knew my course well. For a few minutes, my adrenaline kept pumping from the panic I'd felt, but it slowly subsided, leaving me wet, weak, and very scared.

But not even getting lost on the streets of Washington was as frightening as some other developments I couldn't bring myself to confess to anyone.

I'd always been careful about my appearance—hair, make-up, weight—the whole works. But now when I went for my afternoon run, I'd hurry back to my room, and instead of showering, I'd just tie my sweat-damp hair back, pull on a raincoat over my old sweat suit, and head for the library to study.

One day I looked in the mirror to see that my neglected permanent had turned my hair to frizz. And splotchy skin covered the hollow-cheeked face that stared back at me. *You've got to be going crazy,* I told myself. *You can't even take care of yourself anymore.*

Something else that scared me revolved around my first theology test.

Brian McNealis, a sophomore cross-country teammate, helped me study the Old Testament material the test would cover. Technically, it was just a quiz. But because it was my first college examination, I wanted to do well. So for three days ahead of time Brian drilled with me, going over and over the names of the kings we'd studied, the dates of their reigns, and the basic geography of their territories. I couldn't seem to remember anything.

"You know the stuff, Mary," Brian encouraged me. "Just take it easy and relax."

On the morning of the quiz, I walked down to the language lab, a couple blocks off campus. I got lost on the way, and when I got to the lab, I discovered I'd left my ID back in my room. By the time I returned with the ID needed to check out the audio equipment, I was so flustered I couldn't get the tapes to work right. When I finally asked for help and got through my language assignment, I looked at my watch. It was too late for the Old Testament exam.

I couldn't believe it. I'd been ready, and I'd blown it.

Embarrassed, upset, and worried about the implications of missing the test, I went to my professor's office to apologize and ask what I could do. The professor, Father Walsh, who had known my Uncle Ellis for years, couldn't have been more gracious. "Don't worry," he said. "You can make it up tomorrow, here in the office." So we set a time and I had another night to study.

When I walked into Father Walsh's office the next day, he

showed me a seat, handed me the test, and told me he'd be back in half an hour. I glanced over the first page of questions and my mind went completely blank.

To keep from panicking I went to the window and stared out over the campus where a spontaneous game of touch football had begun on the lawn. All over the campus I could see students moving about a collegiate world that was out of my reach. The life outside the window made my own world seem so small, so confining. And it did nothing for my memory of Old Testament facts.

When I finally turned around to look at the test questions once again, I noticed a map of the ancient Middle East hanging on the office wall. A quick review of that map gave me the answers I needed for the geography-related questions on the test.

There were still a lot of blanks on my paper when I got through. Then I thought about the text and notebook I'd left in the next room. No one else was in the office suite at the time, so I finished the test with a half-dozen quick trips to check my notes. When Father Walsh returned, I was waiting right where he'd left me. I handed him my paper, hurried out of his office, and headed for my dorm—utterly ashamed of myself. On top of everything else I'd lost since arriving at Georgetown, now I'd lost my integrity.

The team went to supper as a group after practice each night. But the nights Mary arrived late, they'd be gone before she got back from her solo run. And she'd miss supper.

But by this time Mary's obsessive thoughts of food were becoming so intense she actually welcomed an excuse not to go to the cafeteria. She adopted the irrational hope that not eating would mean she'd eventually be able to think of something other than the last thing she ate. Of course, with the physical requirements of daily cross-country workouts, the strategy was doomed to failure.

By the time she skipped two or three meals, she'd be so ravenous that the mere sight of a vending machine would send her off on an almost insatiable quest for food. She'd hurry to the nearby convenience store and buy a giant bag of M&M's or a big bag of cookies and wolf down the entire package. Then she'd feel guilty and promise herself it wouldn't happen again. But it always did.

Some days I'd head for practice right after stoking up on junk food. But the steep hills of Georgetown would drain every ounce of energy from my lifeless legs. My head pounded, my stomach churned, and I'd fall far behind my teammates. By this time I'd given up any hope of sticking close to Pia. I just wanted to make it through each practice without dying.

Still, I'd get so desperately hungry. I remember lying in bed with the lights out one night, listening to my roommate's breathing. When I felt certain she was asleep, I slid quietly out of bed and tiptoed to the refrigerator. But when I opened it, there was nothing but one apple, her last one. I snatched it up, crept back to my bed, pulled the blanket up over my head to muffle the sound, and ate that apple right down to the core.

Another evening, when my roommate was out, I became so hungry I opened a box of hot chocolate mix. Ripping open the envelopes, I stuffed the powder into my mouth with both hands. I was still licking the last of the chocolate off my fingers when my roommate opened the door to find me sitting at the desk with the evidence in front of me.

"What are you doing?" she asked.

I mumbled some lame explanation about a craving for chocolate and promised to buy her a new box of cocoa mix. She didn't make a big deal about it, but she had to suspect something.

Another time, when I found nothing to eat in our room, I walked up and down the hall, knocking and checking doors for an unoccupied, unlocked room where I might find something to eat. I'd spent all my cash on junk food and I had to have something to calm my stomach. After searching awhile with no luck, I walked into the darkened room of two girls I barely knew. On their window sill sat a partial loaf of French bread.

I grabbed the loaf and began tearing off chunks of bread and stuffing them into my mouth as if I were some starving animal. There in that room, under the cover of darkness, as I chewed and gulped down that dry bread, an awful sense of fear and guilt washed over me. *What would people think if I were caught?* I knew the answer. If someone had walked into the room at that moment, she would have seen the pathetic figure of a madwoman who had now lost all sense of self-respect.

Perhaps it was a subconscious desire to atone for her sins. Maybe it was another desperate quest for help. But on one of her afternoon runs, as Mary passed a convent not far from the campus, she stopped and knocked on the door. She told the nun who answered that she'd like to know how she might go about joining the convent. The nun invited Mary in and called the mother superior, who came and talked for a while. When she learned Mary was a Georgetown student, the nun told her the first thing she needed to do was finish her studies and then, if she were still interested, she should come back and talk again.

For some time I'd felt worthless to my family, my team, and myself. Walking out of that convent, I felt worthless even to God. I didn't think I could sink any lower than I felt right then. But I was wrong.

Chapter 15

Week followed grueling week. None of the problems seemed to get better. I kept running respectably in cross-country, scoring points for the team, which is probably why no one seemed to notice my weight dropping lower and lower. Finally I hit 85 pounds.

In early October I was looking forward to a cross-country meet scheduled in Williamsburg at William and Mary College. The night before, I'd been in the library late and overslept the next morning. When I woke up and looked at my clock, I was horrified to see that it was 8:05, five minutes after the team was supposed to have left for the meet.

Throwing on my running uniform, I jammed an extra sweat shirt in my gym bag, and raced out of the dorm to the parking lot. No van. I couldn't believe it. *They must have left without me.* Then I saw my roommate, Colleen. "Where's the bus?" I called.

"It left at eight o'clock, Mary."

"Aren't you going to the meet?" I asked. Colleen was on the team, but she'd been out for a couple of weeks with an injury.

"I'm riding down with my mom. It'll give us a chance to talk." Her mother had flown to Washington to visit Colleen over the weekend.

"Can I please ride with you then? I don't know how I missed the van!"

I could see by the trapped look on her face that she would have preferred to have her mom to herself. I didn't blame her. Who would want a weird roommate tagging along? But she didn't have much choice, since my request was certainly reasonable under the circumstances.

"Okay." She shrugged. "You got your stuff? We're ready to go right now."

"I'm all set." Five minutes later we were on our way and I was making strained conversation with my roommate's mother.

When we reached William and Mary after our two-hour drive, I thanked Colleen and her mother for the ride and bolted for the clusters of runners gathering near the starting line. My adrenaline was pumping. What if I hadn't gotten there in time? But I had.

My coach looked up as I pulled to a halt beside him. "Glad to see you could make it," he said matter-of-factly, with only a trace of sarcasm. "We're about to start the race; everyone's already walked the course."

That information alarmed me. "Don't we have time for me to take a quick walk-thru? I don't know this course at all."

"No time," he responded. "Just follow whoever's ahead of you. There shouldn't be any problem."

"What if I want to win?"

He rolled his eyes as if he thought I was joking and began to walk away. "Don't worry about that. Worry about getting dressed. And hurry."

I barely had time to pull off my sweats before the other runners began moving toward the start. To make matters worse, I opened my bag to discover I'd forgotten my racing shoes again. I'd have to run in the old pair I had on. Despite my distressed state of mind, or maybe because I'd worked up an excess of emotional energy in the course of missing the van, driving to Williamsburg, and fretting over an unseen course, I hadn't felt more ready to run since I'd reached the peak of my form in the middle of summer.

When the starting gun sounded, I sprinted into the lead and left the pack well behind me. *I need to slow down and save something for the finish,* I warned myself. But I felt so good I just kept right on running hard. The course seemed well marked, winding between some fields of corn and then along a wide trail that snaked back and forth through dense woods. By the time I reached the halfway point and looked back, there wasn't another runner in sight. I was all alone in the lead.

When I finally left the woods, the course seemed to circle around a cornfield, but I wasn't sure. I saw a course spotter across the field and called to him, "Which way? Which way?" He was too far away for me to catch his exact words, but I thought he was waving me to the left. So I took off around the field in that direction. Here, the course markers were vague, and when I'd looped completely around the field and returned to the spot where the course broke out of the woods, I saw the second-place girl emerging from the trees. Inadvertently, I had run almost a quarter of a mile extra. Uncertain where to go next, I decided to follow her. We ran alongside the cornfield and out onto a grassy area before I realized I had been running off course the first time around!

By now I could hear the other runners coming out of the woods behind me. What's more, the girl in front of me had entered the chute of spectators lining the crest of the course to the finish. I tried to kick and catch her, but my fast, emotional start and the extra unnecessary running I'd done had drained me of any reserves. Three more runners blew past me with the finish line in sight, and I staggered in a discouraging fifth.

"Way to run, Mary!" The coach seemed pleased with my placement.

"But I . . ." I gasped for breath. "I should have won. If . . . I hadn't gotten . . . lost. I ran clear around the cornfield . . . by mistake."

By the time I choked out my attempted explanation, the coach was off to congratulate someone else, leaving me to cry in frustration.

"Mary, great race!" "Hey, Mary. Don't feel bad. You did good." "Did you ever take off at the start!" My teammates' encouraging words were small consolation.

The first couple times I tried to explain, nobody seemed to be listening. *Maybe they don't even believe me,* I thought, feeling a wave of helpless anger. Still I could hardly believe the strange turn of events myself. After almost missing the race altogether, I'd practically won it. Then I'd lost it through a freakish accident. In a few short hours my emotions had see-sawed so many times that I felt completely wasted. And there was no one to blame but myself.

Sick, weak, and embarrassed, I climbed into the van for the long ride back to campus, but what I really felt like doing was going off somewhere and dying. Ever since my arrival at Georgetown, I had prayed things would get better. Apparently, not even God was listening.

The next day, when Mary talked to her folks, her dad told her about an interesting book he had read and made her promise to find a copy of Hilde Bruch's The Golden Cage *in a local bookstore.*

Since she knew she wouldn't be able to read it, Mary didn't even make an effort to locate the book. But after finishing his copy, Leon Wazeter was so convinced Mary's symptoms pointed to a recurrence of anorexia nervosa that he bought an extra copy to give to her coach. And the next weekend, the Wazeters headed for Washington to see about getting Mary in to see a doctor specializing in eating disorders.

One look at Mary after they arrived at Georgetown confirmed her parents' worst fears. Physically she looked as weak as she had the previous winter. But what startled them even more was her emotional and mental listlessness. She walked, talked, and looked like a zombie. The life, the spark that had been Mary, was gone.

Mary's condition so alarmed her parents that they took her along with them to spend the night at a relative's house across the river in Mannassas, Virginia.

I could see the pain and alarm in my parents' eyes the moment they saw me. I knew I was in bad shape. But now at least someone else knew how bad.

"I just want to go home," I begged, desperately needing to be somewhere familiar. Where I'd be in control. Where I'd be Mary Wazeter again. The old Mary.

"Even if you did go home, we'd still need to find some answers to the problem," Dad said. "You'd need special counseling and you'd have to drop out of school. But if we can find the counseling for your anorexia you need here, you can stay in school." He told me they had made an appointment for me the next morning with a specialist.

"Okay," I said. I had absolutely no desire to stay in school and endure another day of despair. But I also knew going home wouldn't be an instant answer either. All my old friends would be gone. High-school life was over. So even the "familiar" wouldn't be familiar. And the old Mary wouldn't be there either. She was gone. Dead, maybe.

"I'll go to the specialist tomorrow," I agreed. I didn't have enough strength to disagree.

I spent an awkward evening at our relative's house. Since not eating supper would call more attention to my problem, I went running first to burn off my excess energy. I was hungry enough to eat a big supper, but was aware that through the entire meal Mom and Dad were casually but carefully watching my every bite.

After dinner, while Mom helped with the dishes, I went into the living room to work on a paper I was planning to write. When Dad joined me a few minutes later, I told him I wasn't able to concentrate enough to get anything out of the material I was reading.

He reached for the book in my lap and, reading aloud a paragraph at a time, tried to explain the meaning. Still nothing sank in.

I finally gave up and went to bed. I couldn't sleep. I thought about the fiasco I'd made of school. I thought about all the dreams I'd had. I thought about the William and Mary race. I thought about my teammates. I thought of my parents and all I'd put them through. The phone calls. This trip down to try to help me. I thought about the prospect of seeing this specialist. I thought about the hopelessness of it all. And I thought about food.

I felt a craving for food.

The house was silent. Dark. I slipped quietly out of bed, opened my bedroom doorway and walked stealthily through the hall and down the stairs to the kitchen where I turned on the little light over the stove and opened a cupboard. Jackpot. A package of Danish.

I tore open the cellophane and broke off a bite just as my mom startled me by stepping into the kitchen. "What are you doing?"

"I was just feeling a little hungry."

"Well, cut a piece of that Danish. Don't just use your fingers."

Minutes later I lay sleeplessly in bed, remembering another darkened house, another midnight kitchen raid back in August when I'd gone to the Falmouth roadrace. At least then I'd asked permission for my piece of pie. *Now I'm stealing food without saying a word to anyone!* The thought was horrifying. How could I have fallen so far in two short months? Like the executioner's song, the words assaulted my mind until I finally fell asleep: *There's no way out. I can't go on. There's no way out. I can't go on.*

When morning came, I had changed my mind about seeing the doctor. There didn't seem to be any point. "I just want to go home," I told my parents. But they were determined to keep the appointment.

We went to church first. I sat through Mass, wondering why I was there. *I'm going to hell now anyway. There's no hope left.*

On the expressway drive into the city, I came to the realization that the only way out was to die. But how? As I watched the terrain whiz by outside the window, I thought, *I could do it right now. I could open my door and . . . But what if I was just injured?* It didn't take long to consider my options before slowly easing the door open.

"What's that?" Dad exclaimed, hitting the brakes and pulling quickly onto the shoulder. I didn't answer. Dad knew. I could see how shaken he was. And Mom climbed into the back seat beside me, clutching me tight for the rest of the drive.

The appointment with the psychiatrist didn't take long. He asked Mary a few basic questions, got some background information from her parents, and announced: "I recommend immediate hospitalization. Not just to get her weight back up, but because I believe she's in danger of taking her own life." The diagnosis he wrote on her file labeled Mary anorexic and psychotic. And he recommended Georgetown University Hospital.

My initial reaction was, *Oh, I'm finally going to get some help.* But that was almost immediately eclipsed by my second thought, *What is everyone going to think? Mary Wazeter cracks up and needs psychiatric care.* Remembering how little help counseling had been so far, I made no response to the doctor's suggestion.

My parents drove me from the doctor's office straight to the hospital where we parked and walked in together. At the admissions desk, my dad did the talking and filled out the preliminary papers. We were asked to wait.

"I don't want to stay here," I told my folks. "This isn't going to help."

Dad spoke up quickly and a little sternly. "You're being closed-minded, Mary. If you want help, you can't do that. This is a wonderful hospital with a good reputation. They'll be able to take good care of you here until you're able to go back to school. And you'll be right here at the edge of the campus—"

He sounded convincing. Maybe he was right. *If I have a good attitude, maybe they'll be able to work out the problem and I can get back to school, back to running soon.*

An aide came and led us to an elevator. We walked in behind her, she punched floor "5," and we all waited in silence until the doors opened once again.

I could feel my good attitude begin to dissolve as the aide pulled out a key and unlocked a heavy yellow door.

The hallway quickly filled up with curious patients wanting to see who had come in. I looked around, noticing that many of these people looked just like I would have expected psychiatric patients to look. Penetrating stares. Strange smiles.

"I'm not staying here," I said, shivering as I felt the goosebumps on my back.

But my dad launched into a pep talk about not being a quitter. And I knew it wasn't my choice.

My parents went with me to my assigned room and Mom unpacked the little suitcase crammed with a couple changes of clothes, my bathroom kit, and a small cosmetics case. An aide confiscated everything but my clothes. She even took the hairdryer, explaining that I could earn the right to use it from time to time.

As she left, I plopped onto the bed in a daze, thinking about the day just five weeks before when Mom and Dad had helped me move into another room. And wishing I could erase the last five weeks of my life. Or maybe just erase my life.

When Mom finished arranging the clothes in a drawer, she and Dad hugged me and said their good-bys.

"Don't leave me."

They said they had to. I followed them to the end of the ward, begging them to reconsider. "Please don't leave me here. Let me go back home with you."

But they walked out. The door slammed shut. And I was all alone again.

Chapter 16

Only months before, my world had seemed so big, so bright, so full of promise. I'd run and won my first international race in Aruba, was looking forward to the trip I'd won to Portugal, and had left home for college, expecting to expand my horizons in new directions.

But the instant that psych ward door locked, my big, open world snapped shut like a steel trap. Gone were the distant horizons, the challenging mountains to climb, the new territory to explore. Suddenly, my world was a hallway, a few hospital rooms, and a cast of bizarre characters I wanted to avoid.

From the window of my hospital room I could see a little of the Georgetown University campus. A couple buildings. A few sidewalks. A half-dozen trees with turning leaves, announcing the progression of fall, of cross-country season, of life. So even this tiny glimpse of my old world—framed in steel bars—served as a harsh reminder of where I was and where I couldn't be.

It wasn't merely the walls, the barred windows, and the locked door that gave me the feeling of imprisonment. The hospital rules and routine seemed designed to deliberately strip me of my basic freedom. Not only had the nurses confiscated all my electrical possessions—my radio, curling iron, and hair-dryer—but I was also a prisoner to the daily schedule required of every patient on the ward.

The first morning, breakfast was served in my room. But I wasn't hungry. I stirred the eggs around a little, nibbled off a couple small bites of toast, downed a few swallows of orange juice, and re-covered my tray. Shortly after the trays were removed, one of the nurses came to escort me to my very first group therapy session.

When she introduced me to the group, I tried to smile. But I remained silent because I didn't know what to say. I knew nothing about group therapy; I didn't even know there was such a thing. It didn't take long to figure out that the patients sitting in a circle were expected to talk about their feelings and their problems. *No way!* I thought.

The whole thing seemed so strange, so strained. Not one of the patients looked like they wanted to be there. Even the staff people sat stone-faced, enduring the silence until someone spoke up. "I'm feeling better today than any day since I tried to commit suicide," ventured one patient. As she went on talking, and as others began to speak up, I realized that several people here had made serious, and in a couple cases repeated, suicide attempts. I was surprised and felt a little awed by them. I wasn't sure I would ever really have the guts to try it.

Finally I mustered up enough nerve to explain why I was there. I told the group about my difficulty concentrating on schoolwork. I admitted to feeling depressed, but I didn't mention my own thoughts about suicide or my eating problems. For a while I felt obligated to say something, to participate in the program. But I had not one ounce of hope that talking about my problems in this group would help.

These people weren't like me. Not one was a runner. Not one mentioned anything about obsessive food thoughts or eating problems. Besides, I was talked out. I'd already talked about my problems to Judy, to my parents, to Pan, to the campus psychologist. And if they couldn't help, what good was a bunch of crazy people going to do?

Then came lunch. I took my tray to the day room where most

of the other patients were eating. I introduced myself to a handsome young guy who looked to be in his twenties and tried to carry on a normal conversation. I knew I was being observed by the staff to see how I fit in, so I obliged.

After lunch came art therapy. The assignment for the day was to paint a picture of trees and then explain why you chose the particular form and colors you did. No one expected me to accomplish much the first day, but the therapist did want to know what kind of art I liked best—painting, knitting, woodworking, ceramics. I told him woodworking sounded interesting, but the truth was I'd never liked art because I'd never been very good at it. Besides, I didn't see how it could possibly solve any of my problems.

Then came the therapeutic dance class. "Everyone imagine you're floating on a cloud. Reach high into the sky—" Again I thought, *What's the point?*

"Free time" was the hour in which patients had regular individual appointments with the staff psychiatrist. I explained to the doctor that my big problem seemed to be my inability to concentrate. When he asked what explanation I had for that, I shrugged. "Just lazy, I guess."

He asked some questions, and we talked about my loss of weight. I was a little surprised that he never used the term *anorexia.* He explained some of the hospital procedures, adding that I could earn pass privileges to leave the hospital. I learned that meant I could visit the campus, accompanied by an aide, or even go out to run if I showed a cooperative attitude in my therapy . . . and if I began to eat. He emphasized the importance of eating more. In fact, the doctor seemed so reasonable and confident that I'd find the help I needed here that I began to hope he was right.

At supper, I ate more than I'd eaten at any meal for weeks. Suddenly I really wanted to get better.

That evening my parents came back to visit. I voiced my

uncertainty about wanting to stay. But my dad repeated his "Give it a chance" speech, so I gave up.

I went to bed after my first full day as a patient with very mixed emotions. I still didn't want to be where I was. But I did want to believe that I might find some help in this place.

Still, the frustration of the forced routine quickly eroded my hope and fed my resentment. Group therapy was the worst. Day two, day three, and day four were all the same. The patients would sit in a circle and one of the staff people would kick things off by asking, "What do you want to talk about today?" I just listened.

A med school dropout talked about stress and her depression. One woman who was obviously psychotic talked about the voices she heard. Several patients spoke of suicidal feelings and their past attempts to end their lives.

I couldn't bring myself to talk about my problems. For one thing, they were too personal to share with a group of strangers. Secondly, I saw no point in going through the pain of public confession when no one in the group seemed to have even a remotely related problem.

For the rest of the day, I was polite. I forced myself to talk to the other patients. I even feigned cheerfulness as I worked on my wooden birdhouse in art therapy. But I always sat, silent and unresponsive, in group therapy.

The one area in which I fully cooperated was eating. I began by eating everything on my tray, every meal. But it was never quite enough. On the third day, after I finished my lunch, I asked the man across the table from me, "Are you going to eat that muffin? Can I have it?" After that it was a regular mealtime routine for me to ask around, "If you're not going to eat your pudding, I'd like it." "Don't you want that cake?" "How about the other half of that sandwich?" After months of self-denial, suddenly I couldn't seem to get enough to eat. My weight began to climb almost a pound a day.

The doctor viewed this change as a positive sign. In addition to that, the staff was encouraged by my willingness to receive visitors. Though my folks had to go home to Wilkes-Barre, Judy stopped by to see me almost every day. And many nights after supper one or more of my teammates or friends from the dorm would drop over for a visit. Whenever anyone showed up to see me, I put on a cheerful face and laughed and joked with them. I had my books with me, so I asked about assignments. And for the first few days I pretended to study, though I still couldn't concentrate enough to read.

At first, I was embarrassed to be in a psych ward. But my family and friends couldn't have been more supportive and encouraging. My folks called regularly, and I found myself deluged with dozens of get-well cards from friends back home and old high-school chums at other colleges. David and all the gang at his school sent notes; I got a letter from Bob, and his folks sent flowers. All of them seemed to echo the sentiment of a friend who wrote: "Mary, you're tough. You've pulled yourself out of so many things before. I know you're going to pull yourself out of this one."

I wasn't so sure. I found myself wishing I had some physical illness that could be treated with drugs or surgery. I'd be able to take the treatment and go home, knowing exactly how long recovery would require. For my problem, there weren't any easy or predictable answers. In fact, I wasn't even sure I was getting better.

I kept acting as if I believed it was all just a temporary problem and that I'd be back in school just as soon as I could get a handle on my concentration problems. At least, that's what I told my friends. But the truth was, I didn't believe it at all. During the first couple days in the hospital, I'd been given some tests—sequential reasoning tests, plus fairly basic standardized intelligence tests. I realized I couldn't answer questions that would have been no problem at all the year before. I was losing the power of my mind, and there seemed to be nothing temporary about that.

I was eating now. Supposedly that was progress. But whereas I'd been eating too little for so long, I was suddenly eating too much. After breakfast, I'd check out the supplies in the ward refrigerator. One morning I cleaned out nearly a whole quart of ice cream. Another day I found a chocolate cake on top of the refrigerator and started gobbling it down by the handful, stopping only periodically to lick the frosting off my fingers. Still another day I finished off most of a plate of brownies the staff had planned to hand out for an afternoon snack.

Each time I pigged out, I'd slink back to my room and lie in my bed, feeling bloated, sick . . . and guilty. But I couldn't control myself. The staff quickly caught on and quit storing goodies where I could find them. But that didn't curb my hunger or my binges.

The first morning I discovered the refrigerator empty, I felt so hungry that I looked up and down the hall to make sure no one was watching and then nonchalantly ambled over to the meal cart, which was waiting to be returned to the kitchen. Then, checking again to make sure no staff members were in sight, I began lifting covers and picking out the leftovers from the breakfast trays of other patients. I was like a vulture, devouring the best morsels before a competitor could rob me of my find.

"Mary! What are you doing?"

When I heard the nurse's voice, I whirled around, trying to conceal a partially eaten piece of whole wheat toast behind my back. "Nothing," I replied.

But I knew she'd seen me. And I flew to my room in embarrassment, knowing she'd tell the rest of the staff and they'd all know there was something drastically wrong with me. I knew it and that incident forced me to admit it to myself. I was just as obsessed with food as I'd ever been. If anything, I was getting worse, because I no longer had the self-control to save myself from total gluttony.

Mary continued to try to present an upbeat front to her family and friends. But her discouragement and her embarrassment only added to her resentment toward the hospital, its staff, and its routine. In group therapy she grew sullen, refusing to respond when spoken to. She began to pick at her fingers with the sharp end of her earrings, poking under her nails until her fingers bled. While fellow patients discussed their problems in therapy, she sat and picked. Even when they begged her to stop, she kept right on, seemingly oblivious to their discomfort or their pleas.

One day Mary locked herself in the bathroom and refused to go to group therapy. When the aides finally broke in, she was sitting calmly picking under her nails. The staff put her on suicide watch, keeping her under surveillance at all times. Even at night a nurse would check her room and shine a flashlight in her face to make sure she was really sleeping.

As I became more and more discouraged, my attitude toward the other patients gradually changed. I'd been so critical when I first entered the hospital, looking down on the others. But now that I'd known them a few days and had seen my own behavior becoming more peculiar, I found myself thinking: "I wish I had his problem" or "She's more normal than I am." I felt particularly compassionate toward one young woman who walked up and down the hall, mumbling and moaning. When I learned from a nurse that the woman's mother had been murdered, I went into the hall and walked with her for a time. I tried to converse, but I had no indication she understood or even heard me. And when she mumbled, I had no idea what she was saying. I finally gave up and went back to my room feeling full of pity for her, but also for myself. *At least she doesn't have an eating problem,* I thought.

One afternoon I stood at my window, looking out over the campus. Students were hurrying to their classes. In the staff parking lot, the nurses were making a shift change. And as I thought about all those people in the outside world going about their lives, I felt more isolated than ever. The race was still on.

Everyone else was moving full speed ahead, but I was vegetating. I had reached the point where reading concentration was not my only problem. I no longer watched TV, nor completed any of the craft projects in art therapy. Sometimes I doodled with a pencil, but I couldn't draw anything except tombstones. I might be able to stand and watch the world pass by outside my window, but the bars prevented me from jumping out and ending my suffering.

Friends continued to visit me. One evening the whole cross-country team dropped by. Another day a couple teammates came over to report: "We raced University of Virginia today and a bunch of their girls were asking about you."

I found it harder and harder to be cheerful for my visitors. Their talk about campus, cross-country, and classes, only multiplied my feelings of worthlessness, and their normality seemed a threat to my increasing abnormality.

Every time a visitor walked freely out the door, I was left imprisoned with the torturing realization of my problems. I knew my behavior was bizarre—the eating, the self-destructive picking, the thoughts of suicide. On the one hand I desperately wanted to get better; on the other, I felt I never would.

All my life I'd tried to be the best, the winner. With every visit from friends, I had to face the fact that I wasn't even in the race anymore. Even compared with my fellow patients, I was a loser. One of them was a professor with a doctorate; one of the younger ones had been in law school. Another, a former commercial artist, painted beautiful pictures in her free time. Others had been married or had had successful careers. I hadn't even made it past the preliminaries in the race of life. I no longer felt pretty or even particularly feminine. I was nothing.

The doctors reported Mary's weight gain to her parents who were encouraged by this small sign of improvement. But the hospital staff also reported her lack of cooperation and their growing concern about her self-destructive behavior.

Feeling hopelessly trapped in a psych ward where she could neither go on with her life nor end it, Mary tried another tactic. She begged her family to let her out.

"I'm never going to get out of here," I complained when Mom and Dad called. "I'm not getting any better. They aren't helping me at all. Let me come home."

Dad lectured. "They can't help you, Mary, unless you change your attitude. You've got to think positively. You've got to cooperate with the staff."

Then I'd switch my ploy from cajoling to accusing. "How can you leave me here? You don't even care about me anymore. If you did, you'd let me come home."

When that failed to budge them, I threatened to check myself out of the hospital.

"You could leave," Dad admitted. "But you'd have an AMA [against medical advice] report in your medical files, and that's a big black mark on your record when it comes to schools, scholarships, and jobs.

"If you'd just cooperate, Mary—" Mom sounded almost as desperate as I felt. "The doctor wants to start you on regular antidepressants. He's sure it will help. Please go along with them, you may be out of there quicker than you think."

I'd seen the movie *One Flew Over the Cuckoo's Nest* and I didn't want to be a drugged zombie the rest of my life. So I'd been refusing the medication.

Since my parents seemed determined to keep me hospitalized, I appealed to Judy for support when she came to visit. "Judy, I need to get out of here. Look how heavy I'm getting," I said, pointing to the tight waistband of my slacks.

"Don't be ridiculous, Mary. You're not the least bit heavy."

I *was* gaining weight from all my overeating, and it *had* lodged around my middle, but I didn't pursue that argument. Instead, I shifted to another issue. "Mom and Dad don't want me to come home," I whined. "They don't care about me anymore.

They want to leave me here even though I'm not getting any help. Let me come live with you, Judy. I know I'd get better a lot quicker than I will staying here."

Judy quickly defended our folks and reminded me that she taught all day and couldn't be home to take care of me. I insisted I'd be fine and wouldn't be any bother at all. But Judy didn't give in either.

In the end it was a call from David that helped to turn the tide. He told me about a friend majoring in psychology who said if I ever wanted to get out, I had to cooperate. He had another friend in pre-med who had explained to him that if my depression was a result of some chemical imbalance, the antidepressant drugs could make a crucial difference. That was a new thought to me. No one at the hospital had explained how or why the drugs might work. Maybe I wasn't going crazy. Maybe there was a correctable problem. I immediately signed the papers to take the medication the psychiatrist had prescribed.

The first day I stood in line for my pills, I couldn't help thinking about Jack Nicholson and all those pathetic people in *Cuckoo's Nest. Maybe I'm going to be standing like a zombie in some psych ward for the rest of my life,* I thought. *Forever.* But I knew I couldn't change on my own. So I took the medicine. And the next day I took another dose.

To reward my new effort at cooperation, I was given my first pass. The antidepressant must have buoyed my spirits because I decided to use my pass to go to the track and run a light workout. Of course, I had to go in the company of an aide. My spirits lifted even more perceptibly as I pulled on my sweat clothes and laced up my running shoes. And they practically soared as I walked across the back of the campus and up the hill to the track. I was finally out in the real world again, breathing fresh air. And I was going to run. I was going to get better and get out of that hospital. I was going to make it.

But two weeks of overeating and inactivity combined with a heavy load of drugs had taken a toll. I hadn't even jogged two laps before I doubled over in pain. Reminding myself that I should take it easy my first time out, I vowed to run again the next day.

The following afternoon, after four short laps on the indoor track, I had to throw up. And I trudged back to the hospital with the realization that I might never run again. All the years of work, all the years of competition were for nothing. My running career was over before it really got started.

The positive boost Mary received from the regular doses of antidepressant failed to offset this new sense of loss and discouragement. And while the staff was cautiously optimistic about her attitude and weight gain, it soon became clear to everyone that Mary wasn't going to recover quickly enough to catch up with her class work by the end of the fall term. Insurance was also running out, so Mary's folks and her doctor agreed it was time to transfer her to a hospital nearer home.

On one of my last days at Georgetown, I used another pass to walk around the campus. Clusters of students clogged the paths that led to the football field, where they were heading for an afternoon game. I recognized a few of the faces. A couple people even smiled and waved. The wind whisked dry, fallen leaves between the buildings and across the walks where they swirled noisily around my feet. I breathed in the tangy autumn air, savoring the smell.

When I reached my dorm, I climbed the stairs to my floor and then walked down the hall to my old room. I opened the door and stepped in. Colleen was gone; she was probably at the game. Her side of the room looked just like it always had. My side had been straightened, my things removed. It was as if I'd never really been there—just a vague memory of an unpleasant dream. And when I turned and walked out of that dorm, I knew I'd never come back to Georgetown again.

When a patient was scheduled for release, the entire ward staged a farewell party the night before. Ironically, at my party, the primary focus was on food. Piles of goodies leered at me from a festive table. There were words of encouragement from staff and fellow patients alike. I tried to smile graciously through it all, but I felt more like hiding than celebrating.

I was going home, not in victory but in defeat. I was heading back to Wilkes-Barre where everyone knew me, where everyone had read my name in the papers for years, where everyone had rooted for me to make it. But I hadn't made it. I was going home in defeat, a total failure.

After almost three weeks of begging my parents to let me out of the Georgetown hospital, when the time came to leave, I didn't want to get in the car.

Chapter 17

I guess my folks remembered the incident when I tried to jump out of the car on the way to the Georgetown Hospital, because this time they brought my uncle to do the driving so they could both devote their full attention to me. Nothing was said, but I could sense their fear, and I felt like some kind of dangerous prisoner being transported from one prison to another.

As we drove away from the hospital and the campus, my folks made an obvious attempt at light-hearted conversation. They tried to include me, but when I failed to respond, the two of them simply talked to each other. I wasn't sure I could stand their feigned cheerfulness for the entire 250-mile drive back to Wilkes-Barre. I maintained a determined, angry silence.

At one point Dad brought up the subject of my weight. "You're looking so much better now than when we last saw you, Mary."

While my folks saw my weight gain as a clear sign of progress, I was disgusted that most of those pounds were still hanging around my midsection. The jeans I was wearing seemed tighter and tighter with every mile—a silent rebuttal of everything my father said and a painful reminder of all that had happened in the past few weeks.

Around noon we stopped at a Burger King just off the expressway. I'd vowed when I walked out of the Georgetown

Hospital that I was going to put my overeating behind me once and for all. But I gulped down a quarter-pounder, large fries, and a Coke before anyone else came close to finishing. So I excused myself to go to the ladies' room. I knew I hadn't eaten as much as I could have, but one look in that bathroom mirror made me sick.

Checking to make sure no one else was in the bathroom, I hurried into one of the stalls, leaned over the commode, and stuck my finger down my throat. I gagged but I didn't throw up. So I tried again; I had to do something to relieve the awful feeling of pressure in my stomach.

As I gagged the third time, the bathroom door opened and I heard my mother's voice. "Mary, are you okay? What are you doing? Are you trying to throw up?"

I didn't have to answer. Any more than she'd had to ask. "Why, Mary?"

I think she knew the answer to that question too, because she seemed very upset by my continued silence. And she didn't let me out of her sight for the remainder of the trip.

As we neared Wilkes-Barre I broke my silence with a single statement. "I want to go home, not to the hospital."

"I'm sorry, Mary, we really have no choice," Dad said, looking sort of trapped. "We're legally required to deliver you to the hospital. You haven't been officially released yet, you know."

"Come on, Mom and Dad. *Please.* I'll do *anything* it takes to get completely well . . . if you'll only let me come home."

But I might as well have been asking for diamond earrings and a new Ferrari. Neither one of them was going to give. So I fell silent again, wondering how my own mother and father could be so mean.

Mary might have pressed the issue harder if she had had any idea what she was getting into. She found the psych ward at Wilkes-Barre General much more depressing than the one at Georgetown. Both were locked wards, but whereas Georgetown had been fairly new, with a bright, open feel, the old Wilkes-Barre ward was small—maybe eight rooms. Even the walls were dark.

The patients were different too. Those in Georgetown had been well-educated, from the upper half of the social strata, while the majority of Mary's new wardmates were from poor- or working-class backgrounds. Most were long-time mental patients who'd been in for so long, or in and out so often, that a hospital routine seemed like home. For many of the patients, this ward was a step up for them; they'd been in the state hospital at Clark Summit and this was the next plateau on their way back to the outside world. But for Mary, this ward was a frightening step backward.

I didn't get off to the best start in my new surroundings. My mood matched the weather that first day—gray and cloudy. Meeting my roommate proved the most traumatic incident of all.

The nurse who showed me to my room pointed out my bed and motioned toward another bed. "That's your roommate. Her name's Rita."

"Hi, Rita," I said, trying to be friendly.

Rita's only reply was a moan.

"She doesn't talk," explained the nurse as she left.

I risked another look at Rita. Evidently she didn't do much of anything. She was strapped to her bed, and all she could do to communicate was to wave her arms and moan.

Just as depressing as the surroundings and the other patients was my first day in group therapy. Even the faces looked different. In Georgetown, the patients had been students and professional people. Here, they wore the worn, vacant expressions of institutional veterans. The stories bore out the differences. Instead of family, academic, and career stress, these patients talked about sexual abuse, drug habits, and mental hospital experiences.

Only one thing was the same—my feelings of futility. Once again I was expected to open up and discuss my deepest feelings with a group of strangers who had little or nothing in common with me or my experience. But I talked, because I was determined to be released. And I was also determined to regain control of my eating habits so I could rid myself of my flabby stomach and get back in shape.

Cooperation paid off. Within a few days I'd earned a Saturday pass to get out of the hospital and spend a day at home. Finally I'd be free, at least for a few hours, from the depressing hospital and its routine.

Mom and Dad picked me up and seemed genuinely pleased to see me. But their conversation on the way home was strained and uncertain. Hoping to relieve the awkwardness between us, I tried to act as positive as possible, noting the familiar streets and asking about old friends.

The first thing I did when we reached our house was to hug my excited little dog, Rusty, and hurry upstairs. Walking into my old room gave me a weird feeling! Though everything looked just as it had when I left for college ten weeks before, it looked somehow different too.

The whole house felt that way. I spent some time just wandering from room to room. Down in the basement rec room, I trailed my fingers across the collection of trophies I'd won and looked at the state medals still in their cases on the shelf Dad had built for them. The pictures of me were still there too. Suddenly they seemed so old.

Mom and Dad were both around all day and we talked some. But mostly they left me to my wandering and my thoughts.

I stayed in my room much of the day. Lying on my bed in those familiar surroundings, my mind flashed back to the time only a year before, when after my first state championship, I'd dreamed about collegiate championships to come. Now all those dreams had become a living nightmare I couldn't shake. Despite the outward cooperation that had earned me my one-day pass, I was fast losing hope that life could ever be happy or good again.

Late in the afternoon, my mom called to me from the bottom

of the stairs. "You need to get ready, Mary. It's almost time to go back."

Something snapped. I couldn't face the thought of going back to that dismal place. Instead of answering, I hid in my closet.

A few minutes later I heard Mom coming up the steps. The door opened. "Mary?" When I didn't answer, she turned and walked down the hall. I knew she was looking in the other two bedrooms and bath. "Mary, where are you?"

I heard my dad come bounding up the stairs to join the search that quickly moved back into my room. "I know she's here," Mom was saying. "She didn't come downstairs."

The closet door opened and I heard the pain in my dad's voice. "Mary! What are you doing?"

"I can't go back."

"But Mary," Mom persisted, "you have to go back."

I sat there stubbornly, refusing to budge from the spot.

"Mary!" My dad used his sternest voice. "You have to come out. Right now!"

I hunkered farther back into the corner.

"Mary!" Helpless frustration replaced the severity of his tone. "You're never going to be able to come home again if this is the way you're going to act."

But the threat didn't move me either. Finally my dad reached in and physically pulled me out of the closet. I kicked and screamed as he literally dragged me out into the room.

"Mary! Please!" Mom tried to help him restrain me, but I latched onto the end of the bed. "I hate you!" I screamed. "I hate you both! I hate myself. And I won't go back to that hospital again!"

The two of them finally succeeded in prying me loose. But I kept screaming, "I hate you! I hate you! I hate you!"

Tears rolled down the faces of both my parents. And my dad, always the optimist, my eternal encourager, my strength, and my biggest fan, moaned, "My God, my God, what are we going to do?" Without waiting for an answer, he wailed out his anguish.

"You're breaking your poor father's heart. We love you so much. But you're killing us, Mary. You're killing us."

Both my parents wept the entire drive back to the hospital, but I didn't shed a tear. My heart was like granite. I couldn't feel anything for anyone, not even for myself.

Back at the hospital again, Mary wavered between determination and despair. As the days passed she slipped back into the binging pattern of eating everything she could find. But she binged discreetly, careful not to let any of the staff see her. In an effort to compensate for the added calories, she began to accelerate her exercise program. When her doctor spotted her doing sit-ups one day, however, he gave her a strict lecture on the danger of her anorexic obsession with weight loss. He told her she didn't need exercise; she needed more Kentucky Fried Chicken.

That incident served as further evidence to Mary that the people at this hospital had no idea what was going on inside her. It seemed absurd that her doctor was exhorting her to eat more when she was already snitching any unguarded food she could find.

Despite her growing skepticism about a medical solution to her problem, Mary continued to cooperate with the hospital staff. She was afraid not to. The psych ward at Wilkes-Barre General wasn't a long-term care facility, and the other patients had warned her that anyone who didn't shape up in short order was transferred to the state mental facility at Clark Summit. If that happened, Mary feared spending the rest of her life there.

Mary was civil to the staff and put on a cheerful front for the Wilkes-Barre visitors who dropped by to see her.

My friend Mark came a couple times to visit and run with me. He was a high school senior that year, aiming for the state title. Since I was off the medication that had weakened me so much at Georgetown, I could run a little better now, but I knew he was taking it easy on me. When we slowed to a walk, Mark talked about his senior season and his goal of state champion. I heard him out, though I felt like telling him, "Look, I made all those goals just last year, but they don't mean a thing to me anymore." Instead, I grinned, encouraged him to work hard, and promised to be out training with him again soon.

But my optimistic façade barely covered my growing disillusionment with psychiatry. I wanted to get better. And some days I even worked up the emotional energy to hope I would get better. But it was looking more and more unlikely.

I tried to psych myself up so that I could get out of the hospital and get on with my life, but I had my doubts. I'd worked all my life to get to the top; now I was at the bottom. It would take so long just to reach "average" again that achieving the world-class status I had attained before seemed virtually impossible. I still wanted to be, *had* to be the best. That was what people expected of me, what they liked about me. And I was afraid I'd never be able to work that hard again. Dying seemed a much simpler solution.

Mary began to think more and more about death, carefully avoiding any mention of the subject in therapy. She knew talk like that would only prolong her stay. And whatever direction her future took—life or death—would be easier to accomplish on the outside.

So Mary worked at being the model patient. She smilingly made potholders and ashtrays in occupational therapy, learned macramé from one of the other patients, and even talked enough in group therapy to avoid the concern of the staff.

The act worked. Just before Thanksgiving Mary was released from Wilkes-Barre General with the understanding that she would continue regular therapy on an outpatient basis at a local community health care facility.

I thought of the old saying "Home is where the heart is" as I walked into my house again. Because my heart felt nothing, I felt sure I could never feel at home again. Instantly I knew what I'd suspected for some time. Release from the hospital wasn't the solution.

Death looked better all the time.

Over Thanksgiving weekend some of my friends came home from college and invited me to go with them to a football game. As they chattered on and on, catching up, comparing college stories, I felt more and more out of place. No one seemed to have any idea what to say to me. Their awkwardness only increased mine. I knew they'd been trying to be nice by including me, but long before the evening was over, I wished I'd never agreed to go. It was another reminder of how much I'd lost, how far I'd fallen. And I woke up Thanksgiving morning, not very thankful at all.

December turned out to be a gray, dismal month. I wandered around all my old haunts alone, freshly aware that life, as well as my friends, was passing me by.

Every weekday I was required to report to the outpatient psychiatric program at the Counsel House. Many of the other patients there were drug addicts, alcoholics, or recent releases from the state mental hospital, trying feebly to readjust to the real world. A year ago I'd have been scared to death of people like that. Now I was considered one of them, required to share my deepest feelings with them and to listen sympathetically to theirs.

My eating compulsion seemed to be getting worse and worse. If my folks weren't watching at breakfast, I'd eat four big bowls of cereal. Before and after my session at the clinic every day, I'd hit the candy shops and the bakeries for all the junk food I had money to buy. *I'm going to die anyway,* I told myself. *I may as well eat whatever I want.*

My weight, of course, climbed until it reached an all-time high of 115. And the heavier I got, the greater my depression until I no longer even pretended cooperation at the Counsel House. I began to pick at myself as I'd done at Georgetown.

I was so sick of talking about my problem that I refused to say anything in group therapy. I'd just sit and dig under my nails until they bled. At home, I stayed in my room and picked at my feet with pins.

Sometimes my mom would come to the door and look in. I'd know she was there, but I wouldn't acknowledge her presence. I'd just keep sticking the pin in my foot, loosening little patches of skin until I could peel them off. Strangely, I never felt any pain. A couple times I heard my mother crying outside my door, but I couldn't feel her pain either.

The one thing that brought me down out of my room was mealtime. Food drew me like a magnet. I ate heartily with my parents, then really gorged when they weren't around.

Periodically I scrounged through the cupboards until I cleaned out everything sweet in the house. My folks didn't confront me about it, but I knew they knew what I was doing. And I didn't care anymore.

One day Mom walked into the kitchen to find me eating dry pudding mix out of a box. Instead of feeling guilty, I glared at her angrily for disturbing me. Then I deliberately finished the last spoonful before I put the empty box on the counter and walked out.

Nothing interrupted my pattern of self-destructive behavior. And the worse it got, the more I felt I deserved the worst that could happen to me. Death loomed closer and closer. It felt inevitable—like taking a class in school and never studying, knowing the final is coming, but doing nothing to prepare for it.

Christmas was pathetic. Everyone came home for the holidays, but our celebration was empty ritual. My emotions had died. Mom even bought all the gifts I supposedly gave, though I still had to go through the motions.

My brothers and sister were obviously distressed about me. I could see it in their eyes. And one night after I went up to my room, the rest of the family held a conference in the living room. No one knew what to do with me. I could hear Judy crying. At one point I heard David say, "Maybe she could go back to school with me after break."

I wished I could run down the stairs and plead for help. But back in August, I'd cried out and no one had been able to help me. Nor had three months of psychotherapy done any good. There just didn't seem to be any solution. Except one.

And as my future was being discussed downstairs, I lay in my bed and thought of happier Christmases. *I had such a nice family.*

But I thought of them only in the past tense. As if my death were already a fact.

The banner in the Wilkes-Barre public square announces the Mary Wazeter Benefit Run, July 1982.

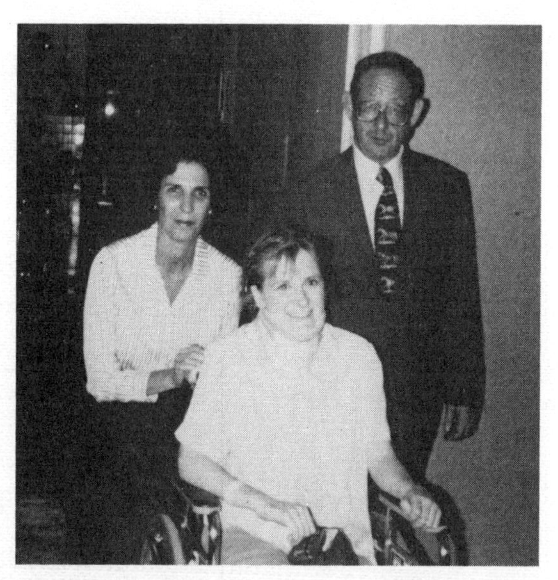

Mary with her good friends Sandy and George at Magee Rehabilitation Center, August 1982.

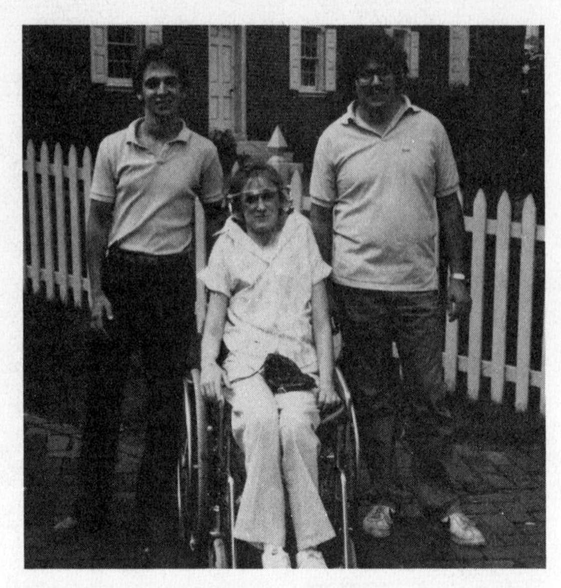

Mary in corrective "halo" while sightseeing in Philadelphia, summer 1982, with high-school friends Nick Mirigliani *(left)* and Greg Baum.

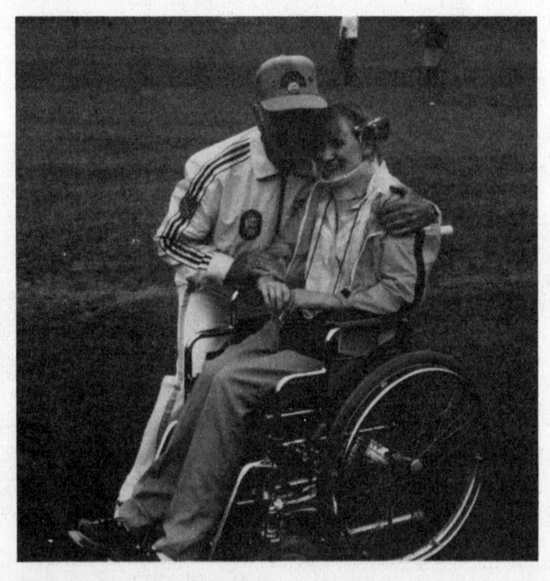

With starter Dinny Nooner

With classmates Andrea Carol and Marybeth Prawdzik on track, September 1982

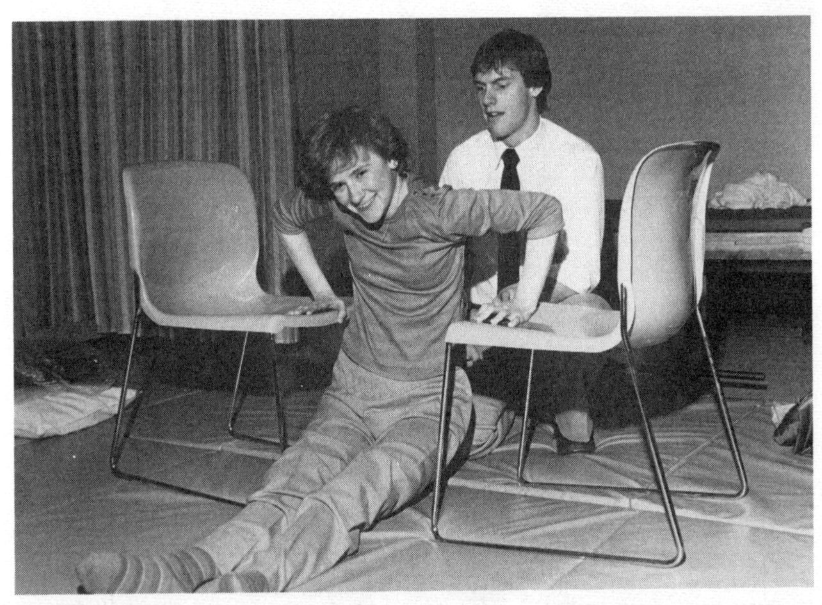

Physical therapist Dave Patrick at John Heinz Rehabilitation Center helps Mary build her upper body strength, May 1983.

With Rusty, July 1984

Mary with Stan Hamilton *(left)*, her neighbor and father of three Penn State football players, and Joe Paterno, Penn State football coach, May 1983

Leon and Edith Wazeter, 1986

With Judy, fall 1986

Getting baptized at the First Assembly of God—Youth Pastor Clay MacTarnaghan *(left)* and Pastor Merv Horst, May 1988

The family: *(from back)* nephew David, Bill and Judy, Sandy and Gerry, David, and Mary, Christmas 1986

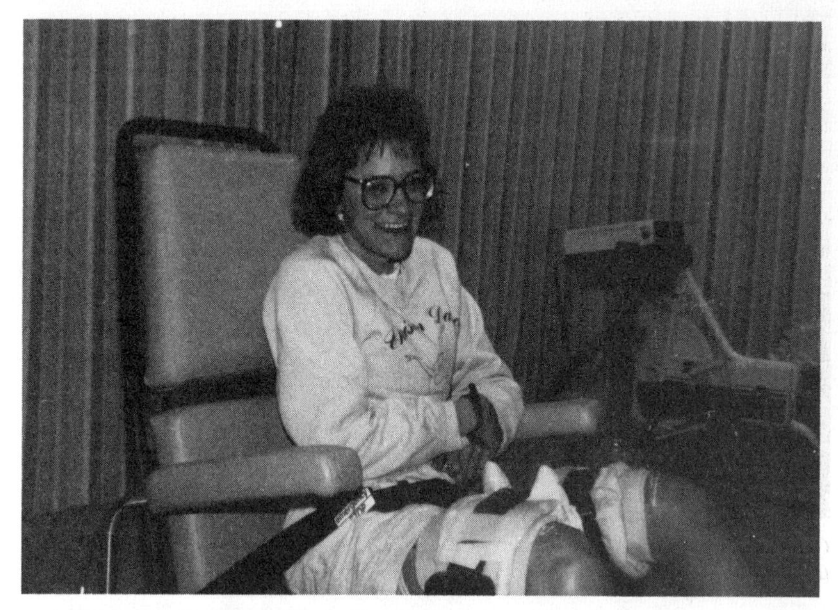

At Allied Services Rehabilitation Center, November 1988

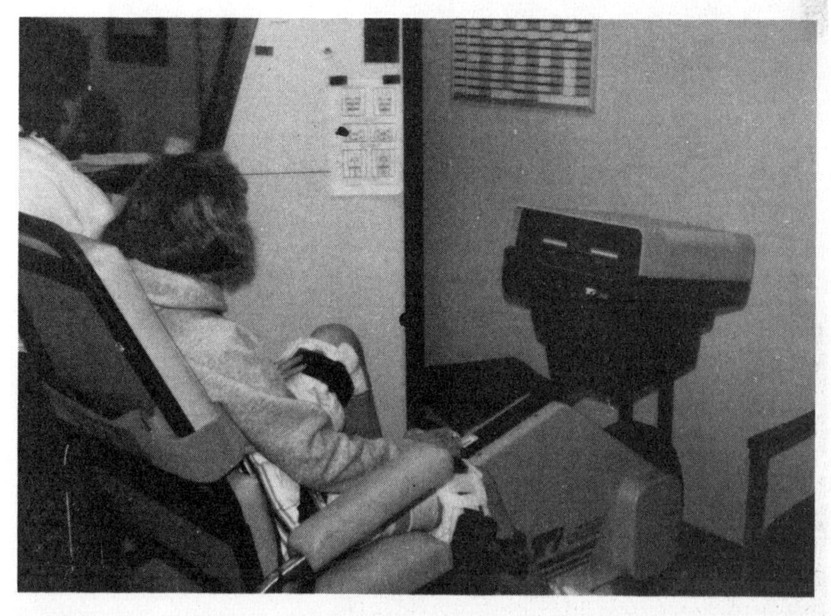

A view of the computer, November 1988

Christmas 1988—*(Left to right; front)* nephew David and Mary; *(second row)* Judy, Leon and Edith Wazeter; *(third row)* Bill, and David holding niece Faith; *(back)* Sandy and Gerry

Chapter 18

For years I had lived for the future, dreaming about the day when I'd achieve all my dreams of a state championship and earn a college scholarship. Even after winning all those races last summer, I was setting new and bigger goals, always looking toward the future.

Once I got to college things soured so quickly I spent most of my time looking back. At school, and then in the hospitals, I longed for a chance to return to my more glorious past, to recover the happiness and sense of victory I'd once enjoyed. I couldn't help wishing my fellow patients had only known me then.

If I learned anything during the course of my psychiatric treatment, it was that I could live life neither in the future nor in the past. I was trapped in the present, with only one clear way out.

I received a party invitation from one of my high-school friends. It was to be a New Year's Eve celebration with a bunch of our former classmates. I couldn't think of a reasonable excuse, so I accepted. But I dreaded the thought of having to face all my old friends again. The contrast between their full, busy lives and my bleak, barren one was just too sharp. So New Year's Eve became my final deadline.

Before I left for the Counsel House on the morning of December 31, I excused myself from the breakfast table. "I have got to brush my teeth before I go." Upstairs, I locked the bathroom door, opened the medicine cabinet, and collected a handful of pills from the assorted bottles I found there. Quickly downing the pills before I brushed my teeth, I hurried back downstairs for the ride to outpatient therapy.

I felt a little woozy throughout the day, but the pills didn't seem to be working. When I got home that afternoon, I went to the medicine cabinet again and emptied several bottles of Avantil, Thorazine, and Sominex. Swallowing them all, I decided to go for one last run.

By the time I reached Kirby Park, I was sure I'd taken enough pills to do the job. My legs were getting heavy and I felt violently sick. While running along the top of the levee, I had to stop. A wave of nausea doubled me over and I threw up. But the relief I felt was only temporary. The heaviness settled in again as I jogged for home.

My legs felt wobbly and I staggered a couple times as I ran along the train tracks and out across the Black Diamond Bridge. *Maybe it would have been easier just to come out here and jump,* I thought. But I kept on running and made it all the way home.

I told my folks I was going upstairs to take a nap before the party. And I lay in my bed, sadly surveying the familiar surroundings as I waited for my final sleep to come.

Two hours passed before Mary's dad went upstairs to rouse her. He called her name from outside her door. But there was no answer.

He called again.

Nothing.

Finally he opened the door and walked in. "Mary." He nudged her shoulder. "Wake up, honey." When she didn't move, he shook her gently. "Wake up."

Mary moaned but he couldn't understand her muffled response. So he shook her more firmly. "Mary! Wake up! What's wrong?"

She rallied to the edge of semi-consciousness, managing to mumble something about pills. Mr. Wazeter now shook Mary forcefully, asking her questions, probing her for details.

Mary's mom hurried upstairs when she heard the commotion. As soon as she understood what had happened, she ran into the bathroom and checked the medicine cabinet. There she found the empty medicine bottles confirming Mary's slurred confession.

Together, Mary's parents carried her downstairs to the kitchen where Mary's dad tried to walk her around to keep her awake while her mother called the paramedics. Only a couple minutes passed before Mary's eyes bulged as if they would come out of the sockets, her body went into violent convulsions, and she slumped into unconsciousness.

From somewhere in the distance I heard voices. I forced my eyes open a crack. It felt like I was lying in the bottom of a deep well, looking up toward a small circle of light. The blurred images of faces peered down into my well, drawing me slowly upward. The circle grew larger until I found myself surrounded by brilliant white light.

Two of the faces hovering above me looked familiar. "Where am I?" I asked, but the question just echoed in my brain. My mouth didn't move. *So this is how it feels to be dead,* I thought. *Or am I dead?*

A few words began to register. "You're . . . okay, Mary. You're . . . emergency room at Mercy Hospital . . . good care of you."

Slowly the events of the past few hours slid into place. The pills. Running in the park. Going to bed. Dad trying to wake me.

The voices belonged to two nurses who lived in my neighborhood. Embarrassment and guilt swept over me as they explained that if I felt a raw, burning sensation in my throat, it was from the tube the doctors had used to pump my stomach.

But I was alive. And for the first time in months, I was glad of it. I'd been granted a second chance at life. It wasn't too late.

Naturally, Mary's suicide attempt greatly upset her parents, but they were heartened by the new attitude of hope they sensed in their daughter and assured her of their love.

By the next morning Mary was eager to go home. The incident meant, however, a mandatory admittance to the hospital psych ward for evaluation. Mary found the mental ward at Mercy the most depressing of any she'd yet seen, so she accepted her family doctor's suggestion that she transfer to the nearby NPW Hospital facility.

NPW was my fourth hospital in as many months. To my surprise, I liked it immediately. The building was even newer than the one in Georgetown, and some of the patients appeared to be around my age. There weren't as many extreme cases on this ward. In addition, the patients and staff seemed friendlier than in any of the other hospitals. So by the time a large, jovial patient had given me the grand tour and introduced me to her friends, I was beginning to think I could actually get better in this environment.

The first morning after a good breakfast, I heard a nurse calling from the hall: "OK. Everyone out. It's exercise time."

"What are we going to do?" I asked as I walked out into the hall.

I found out soon enough. The exercise class consisted of walking—twenty trips from one end of the ward to the other. Moving up and down that hallway, I couldn't miss the depressing irony of it all: six months before, I'd been a world-class distance runner; now I was shuffling along a hospital hallway and calling it "exercise." No matter how much new hope I felt, I had a lot of ground to make up.

Still, I was determined to give life one more try. I cooperated better than I ever had, even going so far as to venture unsolicited information in group therapy about my own case, as well as offering advice to others. My family and friends who came to visit noticed a definite change in me.

And yet, as the days passed, I realized that the doctor and the staff, while concerned about my suicidal depression, hadn't even mentioned my long-time eating disorder. As I ate more and more every day, I realized that I was rapidly losing control over food again. My small reservoir of hope began to erode very quickly after I began stealing the cookies my roommate Martha had just received from her family. Martha was a small, sixty-year-old woman who was always sweet to me, if a little confused. So my thievery shamed me even as I regularly pilfered her treats.

I continued to waver between hope and despair after that. But I never again could escape the sense that I was fighting a losing battle. I kept up my positive front for my parents and my friends on the outside, but I began to talk to some of the other patients about wanting to end my life.

In a few weeks, all but a couple of the patients had been released. Mary was still there.

The psychiatrist assigned to Mary's case gave her an assignment—to write out her feelings in a sort of daily diary. Mary went along with the experiment, recording a wide range of feelings.

The cover of my little notebook bore the straightforward title, "My Journal." On the front I drew three flowers under two subtitles: "The Story of a Girl's Return to Life" and "Battle Against Depression." I made my first entry on Tuesday, January 19:

"Today I woke up and had my usual dead feeling but I forced myself out of bed because it was hard and I enjoyed it. I took a shower and exercised like a normal person starting his or her day and fixed myself up to look attractive. This ritual, however, takes me a long time, I guess because I'm not in a rush to go anywhere. From now on I should get up, be done and ready to sit with the other patients instead of running all over.

"I'm going to force myself to do some regular routine things each morning starting with the rosary, reading some Scripture and meditating on it, shower, then exercise. Also I'd like to write a poem each day along with reading as much as possible. Then there is art and crocheting so my days here should certainly be full ones.

"The future here brings me some excitement. . . I already feel a hundred times more full of energy.

"The best thing is I'm not languishing in the past. It happened and I now see I really couldn't have changed it. I'm looking forward to a long beautiful life filled with friends. I want to stay friends with the people I met here because they have all been so kind. I have too much to be happy about to be depressed and I really mean it."

The next day's entry was four times as long, including my reflections on the departure of Steve, the only other patient who'd been on the ward as long as I. We'd talked a lot and become pretty good friends. I wrote about the warm good-by and then went on to say:

" . . . yet inside [I] felt somewhat indifferent to his leaving. My feelings toward Steve are like mine toward so many people—I become friendly and close in terms of words exchanged and times shared but my inner soul always remains detached. I guess that is why I never experience loss over people as others do, which may have its advantages but on the contrary leaves me a little less human."

My entry the next day followed up those feelings with a poem that read:

I wish I was born with more love
For the people around me and God up above.
They tell me I have so very much to give
But will I be able to really live?
To take the good and the bad and be willing to dare?
To quest for knowledge and perfection of health?
To work hard each day to gain some wealth?
Moment by moment life is passing me by

And yet I stand still unable to cry.
Oh, life precious life, will I ever know?
To be spurred on to tasks that can make me glow?
I'd never give up, I was the girl with the heart.
How did I grow so very far apart?
A family filled with love and joy;
Always caring was a special boy.
But yet I'm living in a world that's cold
Separated from all others, I'm told.
I try and try but just can't connect—
Living alone in my isolated world,
I don't ask for riches or wealth or glory—
Just a feeling of warmth
That wouldn't leave me in a fury.

As the days rolled by, despair swallowed up more and more of Mary's hope. She told one of the staff members about her continuing suicidal thoughts. And though she continued the cooperation charade in group therapy, she resorted to picking at herself again. Her doctor talked to her about the possibility of putting her in a long-term care facility if she didn't show signs of improvement.

Special psychological testing was ordered. In one exercise Mary told stories about a series of pictures. No matter what was pictured on the card, her story revolved around the subject of death. The staff, concerned about Mary's deteriorating attitude, scheduled a meeting to discuss her case. For a time, her parents were requested not to visit, in the hope that a separation might help her.

My earlier cooperation had won me pass privileges to go out for runs with my brother David who was still home on break between terms. He obviously saw our time together as a chance to encourage me.

One day after a fairly long run, he nearly bubbled over with praise: "You did great today, Mary. You know you're really not in such bad shape. If you just keep working at this, I know you can make it." Then he took me to the parking lot behind the hospital and insisted I run a few wind sprints.

To please my brother, I raced back and forth in the lane between those parked cars. But even as I ran, I was thinking, *There's no point to this. Why get in shape when I'm going to kill myself anyway?*

Every night I'd lie awake in bed, trying to think of the best way to end my life. I decided I didn't want to shoot myself. And drugs were out; I already knew how unreliable they could be. The surest, simplest answer was to jump off a bridge. There were lots of them around. NPW was on the side of a mountain, a long way from the river. But if I could get out, I could run to a bridge.

My plan finalized, I went to bed on the night of February 1 and listened in the darkness until everything on the ward was quiet. When my watch said 2:00 A.M., I slipped out of bed and quickly donned the clothes I'd left on my chair. Then I silently laced up my running shoes and stepped to the door to survey the hallway.

I noticed a staff member sitting in the day room at the front of the ward, but he seemed to be watching TV. So I tiptoed out into the hall and toward the back door of the ward, which opened onto some outside steps. Since I'd seen some of the staff come and go by that door, I hoped it might be unlocked.

I paused a couple times in the shadows. *So far, so good.*

I reached the back door undetected and was just groping for the lock when I heard a voice from the day room: "Mary! What are you doing?"

"Nothing," I replied, waiting as the aide walked down the hall toward me.

"You weren't trying to escape now, were you?"

The truth seemed obvious, but I denied it anyway. "Of course not." And I went back to bed, knowing the doors would be watched closely the rest of the night.

Despite that middle-of-the-night escapade and the other evidence of Mary's continued problems, she was discharged from NPW into the custody of her parents on February 2. At the time of her release, the chief of the NPW psychiatric ward told the Wazeters that in his opinion Mary was no longer suicidal, not psychotic, and only mildly depressed. When Mr. Wazeter asked if Mary should be allowed to run alone, the doctor said he thought that would be the best way for her to run. He did advise the Wazeters to continue Mary's outpatient psychiatric therapy, and an appointment was made for another psychiatrist to see her in six days.

So Mary went home with her parents.

My folks and I had agreed I needed something to keep me busy and I'd opted for taking a couple part-time classes at a local business college. On the way home we stopped and registered, with plans to start school the next day.

David called that night, excited and happy about my release from the hospital. "Maybe you could come down to Franklin and Marshall and live with me. You could take a course here."

"That'd be nice," I replied. And I truly wished I could do it. But I knew it was too late.

The next day, I sat with only three other students in a tiny, dreary classroom that looked all the gloomier in the dim light of a gray, rainy February third. I listened as the instructor reviewed a chapter from a text I'd had back in a tenth-grade business class, and I thought again of the superb academic reputation of Georgetown and my classes there in the fall semester.

When class concluded I took the long way home, walking over the Market Street Bridge, through Kirby Park, and then up the path to the railroad tracks and out across the Susquehanna on the Black Diamond Bridge. About halfway, I stopped and looked around at the Wyoming Valley. *This is the place,* I told myself. And I thought about jumping right then and there. But I decided to go home and see my parents one last time.

I wandered around the house for a while, waiting for my dad to get home. Finally I decided I could wait no longer.

I whistled for Rusty, snapped her leash to her collar, and then called into the kitchen where I could hear Mom making supper. "I'm going to take the dog for a walk."

"Be back before supper, dear," my mother called back. "We're having your favorite. Veal parmigiana."

I closed the door quickly behind me and walked out into the night.

Chapter 19

I knew exactly what I had to do. But there was no need to hurry. I walked two doors east to Old River Road and then turned north toward the river. I'd only walked a couple blocks in the dark and the drizzle when an oncoming car slowed down and I looked up to see my dad rolling down a window.

"Mary, where are you going?"

I hoped he wasn't going to insist I climb in the car because of the cold misty rain. "I'm just taking Rusty for a little walk," I replied, holding up the leash for emphasis. "Mom said it'd be okay."

"All right." Dad still looked doubtful. "But don't be too long. It's a miserable night out."

"Okay." I gave a secret sigh of relief as Dad drove away. I'd said my final good-by and was even more determined to go through with my plan. It wasn't so much that I wanted to die, only that I knew I couldn't ever go home again.

Leon Wazeter couldn't help feeling a little uneasy as he pulled away from the curb. He would have insisted his daughter get in the car and go home with him—except for the evaluation of the doctor who'd signed her release from the hospital the day before. The man had been so reassuring, insisting that Mary was no longer psychotic, no longer suicidal, and only mildly depressed. He'd even suggested it would be good for her to get out and run alone.

Despite the professional psychiatric advice, Mary's dad decided he'd try to keep tabs on her—at least from a distance. He looked back for a glimpse of Mary, but she and Rusty were nowhere in sight. His guess was that she had turned down one of the side streets. So he took a right off Old River Road and went around the block, circling back to the river.

When he reached the end of the road at the riverbank, he parked his car, got out and nonchalantly walked up the steps of one of the pumping stations for the city's flood-control system. He stood for a time there on the bank, as if casually measuring the flow of the Susquehanna. Up the river to his right shone the lights of Wilkes-Barre's central business district. Down river to the left, only a few lights dotted the landscape. The dark black span of the D and H Railroad trestle stood out in the lesser darkness of the sky above the river.

After three or four minutes, Leon Wazeter turned and looked back down Old River Road. Still no Mary.

Realizing she must be somewhere on one of the neighborhood side streets, he drove back along Old River Road, slowing at each corner and peering down each street for Mary and Rusty. Even in the darkness he felt certain he could spot her in her white fleece jacket. Finally reaching his own street without seeing a sign of his daughter, he figured she must have headed home and pulled the car into the driveway of his house.

But Mary hadn't come home. Her mom hadn't seen her since she left with Rusty twenty minutes before.

Not wanting to alarm his wife, and reminding himself of the doctor's reassurance, Mr. Wazeter waited restlessly for a few more minutes before telling Edith he was going back out to check on Mary.

Once more he cruised down Old River Road. Turning down one of the side streets, he crisscrossed the neighborhood. A couple times he spotted moving figures in the distance, but when he drew closer, he didn't recognize them. A few minutes of futile driving around was all it took for Leon Wazeter's apprehension to begin to feel like panic.

I don't even know where I turned off Old River Road or what meandering route I followed. I didn't have to think. I knew where I was going, and I knew every house, every inch of sidewalk in the entire neighborhood. Not only had I lived there all my life, but I'd run thousands of miles up and down those streets on smoldering summer afternoons and slushy winter mornings.

Still, I wasn't thinking about the past as I walked. I didn't even notice Rusty tugging and pulling at the end of the leash. My full concentration was fixed on what I planned to do—the bridge, the river. And when I finally climbed the muddy embankment and stood beside the railroad track running along the top of the levee, there were no obstacles left.

Rusty began to cry and whine as I started out onto the bridge. But I merely clutched the leash tighter and dragged her along behind me.

The amplified echo of my footfalls vibrated through the bridge and into the night as I walked along those familiar, worn planks. I kept right on walking until it looked like I was almost halfway across. Then I stopped, dropped Rusty's leash, ducked under the guardrail, and stepped out over the river onto a steel girder. I could feel the beam much better than I could see it in the darkness. But I knew it was only about twelve inches wide and jutted out several feet beyond the walkway. I carefully inched my way to the end.

I wondered how long it would take to drown in the icy waters. But the thought brought no dread, only curiosity. I hoped it would be quick. In planning this moment for the last few days, I'd accepted what I figured was a certainty—that I would go to hell for committing suicide. But I'd told myself it could be no worse than continuing the hell of living. My life was so messed up already that I'd eventually die and go to hell anyway; there seemed no reason to prolong the inevitable and make life miserable for everyone around me.

I was so convinced that, as I stood on that beam, I felt not the slightest twinge of uncertainty. Calmly and silently I counted to ten. Then I stepped out into the darkness, screaming involuntarily as I plunged through the night.

I felt nothing when I hit. My body simply collapsed around my bones like an empty burlap sack. I'd expected the icy waters of the Susquehanna to close over my head, but they didn't. Instead, I felt myself surrounded by a sea of darkness, uncertain why I wasn't drowning.

I could see the blackness of the riverbank and the more distant inky mountains rimming the river valley. A numbing cold penetrated my body. But I could feel nothing else.

There, alone in the darkness, after months of plotting a way to die, I suddenly wanted desperately to live.

Unable to move, certain no one would find me before I froze to death, I cried out, "I don't want to die, God! Please save me!"

Though the words couldn't have reached halfway to the bridge high overhead, instantly I felt a peaceful Presence. *God heard me! I'm going to live!*

After the first few minutes of fruitless searching, Leon Wazeter stopped at his brother-in-law's house, just a couple blocks from his own home, and recruited him for the search. The two of them combed the neighborhood again, to no avail. Mary's cousin joined the hunt, then some neighbors. The Wazeters called the police and an officer told them he'd send someone right down to help look.

Over an hour after he'd last seen Mary, Leon Wazeter spotted Paul McGrane, a former assistant coach of Mary's. He asked Paul to join the search and handed him a battered, weak flashlight, with instructions to check the railroad bridge to see if Mary had gone across the river. Then Leon Wazeter, realizing that there were lots of people out looking for his daughter, went home to wait with his wife.

McGrane, accompanied by Mary's cousin, Gail, climbed the embankment to the tracks and proceeded out onto the bridge's wooden walkway. Every few feet they stopped and leaned over the rail, sweeping the feeble beam back and forth. But instead of water below, they saw only the white surface of an ice floe that had jammed up that afternoon in the giant bend in the river just a short way downstream from the bridge.

Somewhere near the middle of the bridge, thinking he saw a white shape against the ice below, Paul McGrane leaned out over the railing. The light from the flash wasn't strong enough to make out the form. "Mary!" he called. "Are you down there? It's Paul!"

When I came to, I heard sounds on the bridge above. Then a voice. "Mary! Are you down there? It's Paul." I tried to call out, but the words barely carried past my lips.

Then I recognized my cousin Gail's voice. "Mary, we're coming to get you! You're going to be all right!"

At that moment I knew with certainty that God had heard my prayer. And I let the blackness of the night engulf me once again.

The minute the police department took the emergency call, a rescue squad was dispatched to the scene. An officer telephoned the Wazeters to tell them their daughter had been found and that she was alive. Since they knew nothing more, they prayed and waited at home for further word.

Meanwhile, the rescue team arrived at the bridge and paramedic Michael Moyer rappelled down a rope secured to the bridge. He later told reporters what he found when he examined Mary: "She was blue. Her feet were dangling in about six inches of water. Her hips and up were on solid ice. Hypothermia had set in pretty bad. I took my bunker coat off and put it on her."

Within minutes a wire stretcher and woolen blankets were lowered by rope. Then firefighter Donald Comptom rappelled down to help Moyer lift Mary into the stretcher and wrap her in blankets. The two men also agreed it would be safer to take Mary across the ice to shore than to hoist her up and onto the bridge again.

Police and firemen struggled to launch a ten-foot, flat-bottom boat from its trailer, up the embankment, and down into the river. With the first six or eight feet iced over and most of the remainder of the river solid ice, the going was treacherous. Someone tied a heavy rope to the boat, and patrolman Leonard Martin and firefighter John Livingston climbed in and tried to maneuver their craft out to the middle. They shoved the boat much of the way over the surface of the ice, using peavies—long stout poles with a levered hook and a sharp metal end. But the boat kept breaking through the ice, slowing their progress. More than ten minutes passed before they reached the two men who were carefully tending the stretcher under the bridge.

Mary's rescuers carefully placed her stretcher in the bottom of the boat, which moved slowly back toward the south bank as a dozen men pulled on the rope attached to the stern. On shore, Mary was lifted out and rescuers slid her up the steep riverbank where she was loaded into a waiting ambulance and rushed to the nearest hospital.

Leon and Edith Wazeter heard the terrifying, pulsing screams of the sirens as the emergency vehicles raced away from the river and then along Old River Road and off into the darkness. Within minutes, as soon as the phone rang with word that their daughter had been checked into Mercy Hospital's emergency room, they were on their way.

The next thing I remember was the sound of voices. I couldn't see a thing, but I heard people talking. "She was that really good runner," someone said. "She jumped off the old railroad bridge. Why would a young girl want to do that?" "She comes from a nice family and . . ."

Everything faded out on me. It was dark and I felt so cold.

Mary's body temperature had plummeted to eighty-five degrees by the time the paramedics wheeled her through the emergency room doors. So the staff worked to stabilize her metabolism while trying to assess any other immediate threats to her life. Since both lungs had collapsed, they quickly hooked her up to a respirator. The fall had also resulted in six fractured ribs, a broken wrist, and a compression fracture of the third thoracic vertebra.

Mary doesn't remember seeing her parents at the hospital that night, but her dad says she apologized for jumping off the bridge and for causing so much trouble. Neither does Mary remember agreeing with her parents the next morning to allow the doctors to operate on the damaged vertebra.

In the next two days Mary endured ten-and-a-half hours of surgery on her spine to clear away broken fragments of bone and to fuse the vertebra with bone taken from her ribs. When a blood clot developed in her shoulder, she almost died on the operating table. But the surgeons revived her and completed the operation. Mary remained unconscious for most of those two days.

All I remember is a flash of bright operating room lights. Darkness. And pain. Incredible pain.

Chapter 20

I heard strange noises even before I opened my eyes. A hum. A whir. A pulsing sound. Everything seemed muted. But perhaps my brain had turned down my auditory senses in an attempt to make the pain more bearable.

Yet the light shining through my eyelids was so bright that I dreaded opening my eyes. Curiosity awakened with consciousness, however, and when I finally forced a squinty look into the brightness of Mercy Hospital's intensive care unit, the first objects my eyes focused on were the smiling faces of my parents.

The feelings of love and gratitude that welled up inside surprised and nearly overwhelmed me. They were feelings I hadn't experienced for months—feelings I was afraid I'd lost forever.

I felt like Dorothy waking up after her visit to Oz. Everything was real again. Dad was Dad, Mom was Mom. And I loved them again, just like I always had before the past few months.

I tried to tell them; after all I'd put them through, I wanted them to know. But as I moved my lips, I realized I couldn't speak. A respirator tube in my mouth pumped air into my collapsed lungs at regular intervals. Another tube ran through my nose and down into my stomach, while still another tube in my chest drained fluid away from my lungs. My mouth felt dry and swollen. And my insides felt scraped and raw. I continued to move my lips.

"Don't try to talk, Mary," Dad urged while Mom patted my arm. "Save your strength and try to get some rest. You need rest more than anything right now."

"Maybe she could write something," someone suggested.

"But she's left-handed," my mom replied.

And for the first time I felt the cast on my left arm. Judy came up with the idea of using an alphabet board and, as she pointed to the rows and then individual letters, I'd blink or nod to signal my choice. Slowly I spelled out a summary of my feelings: "Glad to be alive" and "Sorry."

My parents nodded, blinking back tears. And when I indicated my legs and tried to let them know I couldn't feel anything below my chest, they were reassuring.

"Since your spinal cord wasn't severed, the doctors say there's every reason to hope that you'll regain the use of your legs," Dad said, adding, "But the swelling has to go down first . . . and that may take some time."

Even that vague warning didn't subdue the rush of gratitude to God who had heard me that night under the bridge. And I closed my eyes and rested.

On my first full day of wakefulness after the trauma, the nurses had me sitting up. But while I felt somewhat encouraged by this progress, the positive feelings were overshadowed by blinding pain from all my fractured bones and the two major surgeries. In a desperate attempt to fill my mind with something besides my own physical agony, I picked up a book someone had left beside my bed. The book was appropriately titled, *When the Going Gets Tough.* A few minutes later, when I realized what I was doing, a new wave of thankfulness washed over me. I could read! And I understood what I was reading!

After months of mental bondage and stagnation, when I'd been unable to shake those obsessive food thoughts, my mind was free. I was free! I could read!

For me, there could be no greater miracle. This was proof that

God had begun work already. And if he could heal my messed-up mind, I told myself, he could certainly take care of the rest of me. My emotional problems had tormented me for so long that I felt certain that any physical struggles would prove minor by comparison. After all, I'd always prided myself on my strength and stamina.

But Mary's newfound optimism was soon put to the test. The alphabet board proved awkward and slow. So she began scratching out messages on paper—with her right hand. She had to write large, and some words proved illegible at first glance. But as Mary's family learned to decipher her scrawl, her right-handed penmanship became steadier.

One of her first notes expressed her determination to live. The oversized words filled a legal-size piece of yellow notebook paper: "I'm the toughest person in this whole hospital."

But subsequent notes, while hopeful, acknowledged the pain. "My mind could endure anything after this. I could study anything." And later: "I can identify with Christ's crucifixion perfectly now. It's harder than any race that could ever be imagined."

I soon learned to live with the pain and to ignore the disconcerting phantom sensations that made it feel as if my toes were being twisted into knots or my legs were sticking straight up or moving all on their own. But breathing on the respirator seemed like endless torture.

When I contracted pneumonia, my condition went from bad to worse in a hurry. I awakened from a troubled sleep to find a doctor bending over me, his hands at my neck. The next thing I knew his fingers were inside my throat, gagging and choking me. Strangling me. I tried to scream, but nothing came out. I struggled as the doctor slid a plastic tube through my neck and down my throat. But nurses held me and tried to calm me with words I couldn't hear. Suddenly it was over. The doctor let me go, and I heard the nurse explaining: "We had to do a tracheotomy so you could breathe, Mary. You'll be okay." But the terror didn't subside for hours.

The trach seemed as much a problem as a solution. From time to time phlegm or fluid would build up in the tube and force me to gasp for air until one of the nurses came to suction me. I had to avoid thinking about the machine, because I had to stay perfectly relaxed to breathe rhythmically at the respirator's preset pace. If I tensed up, I began to choke. It reminded me of swimming and breathing in rhythm; when your breathing gets out of sync with your stroke, you get the same kind of panicky, suffocating feeling.

The worst times were during the daily x-rays to monitor the healing of my lungs. Every morning the nurses would sit me up in bed and maneuver me into position for the x-ray machine. The pain was bad enough, but they also had to unhook me from the respirator until I was properly situated. And every time I went off the oxygen I experienced a terrifying fear of suffocating.

Within days the hospital staff had me sitting up in a Gerri chair, a contraption with wheels and a movable tray. Sitting was almost unbearably painful, but the nurses waved off my protests, insisting that I needed to be in this position to regain my strength and fight the pneumonia. Doctor's orders.

Even worse than the pain was the feeling of abandonment I felt when the nurses would get me situated and then walk out, leaving me slumped awkwardly forward against the tray. Sometimes one of them would forget to leave the buzzer within reach, and I wouldn't be able to summon help until someone looked in on me and I could motion them over.

Another afternoon I was slumped forward in my chair when my parents came in for the two o'clock visiting period. "Oh, Mary, you're up," Mom commented cheerily. "Have you been out of bed long?"

I held up four fingers.

"Four what? Not four *hours?*"

I nodded.

"You must be mistaken, Mary," Dad said. "How do you know?"

There wasn't a clock in the room and I wasn't wearing a watch. I pointed at the radio I'd been listening to. And I knew my folks believed me then because they called a nurse and had me put back in bed. But the doctor continued to insist that despite the pain it caused, I needed to be sitting up. The more, the better.

Many of Mary's injuries began to heal over the next few weeks. But the paralysis continued. And she remained in intensive care for treatment of her persistent pneumonia.

During this time, when Mary was battling both physical and emotional pain, her only real outlet of expression continued to be the notes she scrawled in red ink on yellow notebook paper.

She wrote on February 14: "At times it feels like I'll never get anywhere but I must be patient."

On February 15 she wrote: "Right now all I could want from life is to sleep without pain. Someday I know I will."

Later the same day she wrote about her regrets about the past: "Everything was there just waiting for me. . . . Why didn't I see the light before it was too late?"

On February 20, Mary wrote about her feelings toward food. She remembered: "I used to get up every morning and all I wanted to do was stuff my face." Then, "In the summer I wouldn't touch food unless I had run 10 miles."

She knew she needed to eat and she wrote: "I'm trying but I don't think I'll ever get my old appetite back because of what food did to me psychologically. I now hate even the thought of it. . . . You'll never have to worry about me overeating again."

Later that same day she wrote: "As I feel better I will pray more and give thanks for feeling better. But now it is constant suffering."

A few days after I'd been admitted to the hospital, a few people from a local charismatic Catholic group contacted my father and asked if they could come and pray for my healing. Dad told them he'd check with me, and I gave my okay.

Father Ted Jarvis, a Jesuit priest from the University of Scranton, introduced the people to me and explained that they had come to pray for me if I would like them to. I nodded, feeling a little awkward to be the focus of my own private prayer meeting, but knowing I needed all the help I could get.

The four of them gathered around my bed, placing their hands on my head, shoulders, and arms. And they began to pray. They prayed that the Spirit of God would give me joy to replace my depression. They prayed that I'd be open from head to toe for the love of Jesus to flood my mind, my body, and my spirit. They prayed that I'd be surrounded and filled with a love that would drive out the fear and the self-hatred that had plagued me in the past.

There was a gentleness and peacefulness in their words and their touch that seemed to flow through me. More than anything else in the world, more than walking again, I wanted that special kind of peace to stay with me. I'd known that feeling before—when I'd called out to God on the ice. And now I felt he was in the hospital room with me and wanted to help.

The warm sense of peace remained long after the group left, and I slept better than I had in months. Something else seemed to have happened as those people prayed for me: the constant "Why?" and "What if?" questions that had bombarded me since I'd awakened in the hospital began to fade, in frequency and intensity.

I began to understand what needed to happen. Right away I wrote a note to my folks: "I can't spend all my time living in the past." Yet I also admitted on paper: "I'm suddenly so scared of the future."

Later I expressed my new hope when I wrote: "I know God loves me and I like myself."

Despite some obvious progress, Mary still wasn't regaining movement below her chest and the potentially dangerous pneumonia had not abated. The Wazeters were naturally troubled, but trying to get specific information from the doctors proved frustrating.

One evening Leon Wazeter waited outside the intensive care unit, waiting for the thoracic specialist who was treating Mary's pneumonia to come out and give an update on her condition. But a few minutes after the doctor went into the ICU, Mary's dad saw the doctor exit through a side door and walk quickly to a nearby elevator.

"Doctor! Just a minute, please," Mary's dad called as he hurried down the hall. He caught up with the doctor just as the elevator doors opened. "I want to ask you about Mary."

"I can't talk now. I'm in a hurry."

"I'll just take a moment of your time."

"I'm taking this elevator."

"Then I'll ride with you."

But all the doctor really said before the doors opened and he scurried away was that the medication seemed to be slowly taking effect, and they'd have to wait and see how long it would be before Mary could be released from intensive care.

If possible, Mary's neurosurgeon seemed even more insensitive to her family's feelings. On March 1, when Mary complained to her mother once again about the length of time she was left sitting slumped over in her chair, Edith Wazeter called the doctor. In trying to explain her concern, she told him, "It's like asking Mary to run a marathon before she can run a mile. She just can't sit up for that long."

The doctor's reply was staggering: "Well, she's going to have to get used to sitting. She'll be in a wheelchair for the rest of her life."

Edith Wazeter cradled the phone without saying another word. While the Wazeters knew, of course, that there was a chance of permanent paralysis, this was the first time any doctor had ventured that prognosis. She couldn't bring herself to tell Mary, who was still struggling with roller-coaster emotions.

A week later, discouraged by the fact that she was still in ICU, Mary wrote: "I can't forgive [myself] that I worked for six years for something and in a couple of weeks let my whole life go down the drain."

Not everything was negative. My reading was probably the biggest plus. Even though I was stuck in the hospital, reading made me feel less isolated than I'd felt for months. As long as I could read, I no longer felt as if the world was passing me by.

I read everything I could get my hands on. My parents brought me books. Sister Catherine, a nun who visited me almost every day, brought devotional readings and Psalms. My sister either dropped by or sent cards containing Scripture verses, with instructions to read and reread the portions every day. And then there was a steady stream of mail. Reading not only filled my time and took my mind off the continuous pain, it began to stimulate mental capacities that had lain too long dormant. I was a thinking, reading person again; and that made me feel a little better about myself.

Another great help was all my visitors. In addition to the regular visits of my family, I had over a hundred visitors in those first few weeks. I could only communicate through notes, and visiting time in the ICU was limited to twenty-minute intervals. Even so, friends, parents of friends, former teachers, and people I'd known all my life kept coming by to see me.

I received a menagerie of stuffed animals. At Valentine's Day I'd been flooded with cards. And I remember one day, as my mother read me some of my mail, I was struck by the thought: *I'm not a star anymore and people still like me. Maybe it was* me, *not my accomplishments, that they liked all along.*

And yet, feeling loved wasn't the same thing as feeling lovable. Despite all she'd put herself through, and only partly because of it, Mary seemed to have a harder time accepting the way her body looked than she did her new limitations.

March 9 was a landmark day. Almost five weeks after being wheeled into Mercy Hospital's emergency room, the doctors released me from intensive care and I moved to a regular semi-private room.

But getting out of ICU didn't prove as great as I'd hoped it would be during all those weeks when I thought the day would never come. The pneumonia was almost gone. But the pain hadn't subsided much. And I continued to have to communicate by writing because the doctor wanted to leave the tracheotomy open in case the pneumonia flared up again.

By the end of the second week in March, I finally got the doctor to talk to me a little about the continuing paralysis. I wasn't really surprised. I reported what I learned to my parents in a series of notes dated March 13:

"He didn't come right out and say 'You won't [walk again].' I could tell he was beating around the bush because it sounded like I wouldn't be going to PT [physical therapy], but to a place where they teach you how to live in a wheelchair."

Though my parents weren't willing to accept the prognosis, I was ready. After lying in bed for six weeks, thinking about the past and worrying about the future, I now felt resigned to whatever lay ahead. And later that same day I reported in a matter-of-fact note: "So I have to be sent somewhere where they teach you to live without legs."

All that remained for me at Mercy was to get strong enough to be moved to a rehabilitation facility. The days continued to pass. And on April 1, almost two months into my hospital stay, the doctor finally agreed to take out the trach.

My voice was raspy for a time. But it was like being given back a whole part of my life. I could both talk and eat comfortably again. And one of the first things I asked Mom was, "Could you bring my calorie counter from home?"

Chapter 21

All that I'd been through, all the problems I'd faced because of my distorted attitude toward food didn't keep me from being worried about my weight. Or my appearance.

Once I was out of ICU, I finally got a good look at myself. The stomach muscles I'd religiously toned with years of daily sit-ups had given way to a paunch bloated by medication, inactivity, and hospital fare. The tiny waist I had always prided myself on was a thing of the past. And I poured out my frustration and bitterness to my mom: "How would you like to live with a belly like mine?"

I asked for a mirror, but what I saw when I held it up made me wish I hadn't looked. My face was blotchy and puffy from all the drugs, and my hair looked lank and straggly.

I didn't need a mirror to see that my arms were like toothpicks, making my body seem even more disproportionate. And I asked Mom if she thought my legs were too heavy.

Now, despite the satisfaction that came with being able to talk again, I knew I was a physical wreck. I wondered how many people would have cared enough to write or visit me if they'd known what I looked like. With the lessening of the pain, I finally had the emotional energy to bask in self-pity. Or maybe it was just easier to complain out loud than it had been when I had to write out every word laboriously with my right hand.

Once, when I'd been grousing about everything from the nursing staff to the dim prospects for my future, my parents simply got fed up. "If all you're going to do is wallow in misery, we're going to go on home," Dad warned. And when I didn't make any attempt to cheer up, they did leave.

Later, as my mother and I were discussing the subject of my future, she said, "Whatever happens, Mary, whatever you do, you're going to be an inspiration to others. Maybe more of an inspiration than you ever could have been as a runner."

"Do you really mean that?" I asked, hardly daring to hope she might be right.

Yet I did think God must have spared me for some purpose. I still felt some of that unbelievable peace that had first come to me when I cried out on the ice. And I still felt God was there in the hospital with me.

One of Father Jarvis's friends, who'd come to pray for me right after the injury, came back to see me each week. She sounded a lot like Mom when she said, "God has a plan for your life, Mary." And each week she prayed that I'd be able to forgive myself and discover that plan.

It wasn't that I didn't want to believe her. In fact, from the time I had the trach removed, I told everybody who would listen that God had saved my life. So it wasn't that I didn't appreciate what he had done for me. But there were still so many questions, so much anger and guilt, so much uncertainty. I couldn't seem to escape my growing mood of discouragement.

My sister Judy had already made a number of trips from Virginia to see me in the hospital. But our communication was limited when I'd had to write out everything I wanted to say. I was especially eager to have a normal conversation when she came for another visit at Easter.

Judy was the kind of big sister who said what she thought, without skirting the tough issues. So I poured out my fears and uncertainties to her, openly and honestly, knowing she would understand.

"You know what you need to do, Mary?" she said after my grim monologue. Before I had time to ask "What?" she continued: "What you need to do is turn your whole life over to God—your past, your present, and your future." She went on to explain that it was very simple, that I could do it right there in the room if I wanted to.

When I agreed, she suggested I pray along with her. And as she led me through a prayer, sentence by sentence, sometimes phrase by phrase, I prayed too. I asked God to forgive me, not only for trying to take the life he had given me, but for all the wrong I'd ever done, all the good things I'd left undone. I asked Jesus to come into my life, to live in me and through me. I asked God to fill me with his own Spirit and to begin to change me into the kind of person he wanted me to be.

It didn't take an expert in theology to know that my experience with Judy in that hospital room was what many people call being "born again." What happened that day was real. I felt a definite change which only deepened in the days that followed.

I began to feel God was really listening when I prayed. When I asked him for strength, I could sense his Spirit. I felt I could be totally honest with God, that I knew him and he knew me. The Presence I'd experienced on the ice and in the hospital was no longer just *with* me; he was *within* me.

I'd been reading the Bible for weeks. But now I couldn't get enough of it. Judy sent cards with Scripture verses written on them and urged me to read them every day until I could repeat them from memory. I found real sustenance and inspiration in those Scriptures, verses such as: "My grace is sufficient for you: for my strength is made perfect in weakness" (2 Cor. 12:9), and "I can do all things through Christ, who strengthens me" (Phil. 4:13).

As my feelings toward God changed and grew, my feelings about myself began to change too. I had progressed through a number of stages since jumping off that bridge: anger, confusion, self-condemnation, self-pity, fear, and through it all, guilt. Now, for the first time, I felt forgiveness—God's forgiveness. But as the awareness of his forgiveness began to sink in, I felt the first tangible hope that I might eventually be able to forgive myself too—the way I was. Not the way I had been, or the way I hoped to be someday. If God could accept me as a physically, emotionally, spiritually broken person, then I could learn to accept myself.

I asked Mom if I could have my hair permed and if she'd bring me some colorful nightgowns from home to replace the hospital-issue gowns. I began using makeup again and doing my best to present a more attractive picture to visitors.

Despite some obvious reasons for continued concern about their daughter—her physical health, her emotional struggles, and her request for the calorie counter—the Wazeters viewed Mary's improving attitude and her renewed desire to look her best as two very good signs.

Earlier, Mary's folks had wondered what, if any, damage had been done to her mind. And though she was able to read with comprehension again, weeks had passed in which the only communication they had from her had come in the form of cryptic, scribbled notes. Leon Wazeter, especially, felt the need for added assurance of Mary's mental agility.

A few weeks after Mary was admitted to Mercy, he had an idea he thought would be a diversion for his daughter as well as provide him with an accurate reading of her mental condition. From back issues of Reader's Digest, *he tore pages containing the feature, "Increasing Your Word Power," read the questions to Mary, and asked her to indicate the correct answers. The competition between them cheered him on a couple scores: first, because Mary sometimes beat him; and second, because her competitive spirit seemed to have survived intact. She still didn't enjoy losing.*

But the most telling test Leon Wazeter gave his daughter was after the trach tube was removed. He handed her a copy of the classic book, A Tree Grows in Brooklyn, *asked her to read it and write a book report. Mary accepted the challenge, completing the book in a little over a day, and writing a report that filled two legal-sized notebook pages, single-spaced. (Her left hand was out of the cast and she was writing again—in small, legible script.)*

"When I read her paper with its concise summary of the book's plot, its proper grammar and sentence structure, it's readable flow and logical conclusions," says Leon Wazeter, "I knew our Mary was back. I knew she was going to be okay . . . at least mentally."

Physically, the future didn't look nearly so bright. Mary and her family began serious discussions about where she would go when she left Mercy.

After a few days of light workouts with hand weights, I graduated to regular physical therapy, which meant a daily trip by wheelchair down to PT. But there were no illusions that Mercy could do very much for me. They simply weren't equipped or staffed to train me for life in a wheelchair. Before I could ever hope to go home to stay, my next stop would have to be a rehabilitation center.

After checking the options, we settled on the Magee Rehabilitation Center. And since most of the patients are referred by Philadelphia's nearby Thomas Jefferson University Hospital, the doctors at Magee, my folks, and I agreed that I should be reevaluated at Jefferson. Their Neurosensory Intensive Care Unit is one of fourteen regional centers in the country specializing in spinal cord injuries like mine.

On the morning of April 23, nearly three months from the time I'd arrived at Mercy, my mother gathered the last of my things as we prepared to move out. Nurses and ambulance attendants maneuvered me onto a rolling litter and wheeled me through the now familiar halls of Mercy Hospital.

A small crowd had gathered just inside the emergency room doors—X-ray technicians, some nurses from ICU, orderlies and aides who'd wheeled me around the hospital for the past few weeks. Even the girl who brought me the paper in the morning was there to say good-by. And though I realized I'd made a number of friends among those who cared for me at Mercy, my predominant feeling was one of excitement, not sadness at leaving. The people at Mercy had helped to save my life; now it was time to get on with that life.

As the attendants rolled me out of the hospital and loaded me into the waiting ambulance that would take me to Philadelphia, I got my first breath of fresh air in months—cold enough to make me gasp in surprise. The ambulance doors clanged shut, and I realized once again the uncertainty ahead. But that one lungful of crisp fresh air was enough to buoy my spirits and I didn't look back when we pulled away.

I was still thinking about the future when the ambulance rolled past a big part of my past. Suddenly it was in full view, just outside the window—Meyers High School. To my surprise, there was no pain in remembrance.

The trip took over four hours. But we made it. And the difference between Thomas Jefferson and Mercy was like night and day.

After Mom and Dad checked me in and I met my nurses, I was given a pass to leave the ward and take a rolling wheelchair tour of the hospital. Just seeing this spiffy modern facility gave me a sense of progress. I was even able to take my first couple meals in the cafeteria, set in a beautiful atrium filled with lush green plants thriving under a glassed-in ceiling that gave the whole scene an open, airy, outdoor feel.

But Mary's newfound freedom was curtailed the very next day when the chief doctor of the unit came in to take a look at her. He noted the way her shoulders hunched up around her ears, the way she slumped forward when she tried to sit up, the bend in her back, and promptly ordered her to bed until the staff could run a complete set of x-rays and tests. His diagnosis of kyphosis—an increase in the concave curvature of the spine, commonly referred to as hunchback—told the Wazeters very little.

Jefferson was a teaching hospital, so I soon learned that a patient never sees just one doctor at a time. There always seemed to be a small herd of residents traipsing around after the specialists. I remember one particular encounter after I'd been restricted to bed.

One of the staff surgeons stopped in to see me. He picked up my chart from the end of the bed and summarized the information for his entourage of young doctors: "Injuries took place on February 3. She had anterior laminectomy and posterior laminectomy within a couple days after that. . . . But she's developed a severe case of kyphosis. . . . Hmmm. An automobile accident? No, I see . . . a fall."

He peered at me over the rim of his glasses. "What kind of fall, Mary?"

I took a deep breath to answer, but Mom intervened. "Mary was a victim of anorexia nervosa. She became depressed and tried to take her own life by jumping off a bridge," she said quietly.

"Oh." There followed a long awkward silence as the doctor continued to study the chart. "Has the staff psychologist been in to see her yet?"

I cringed inside at the instant label—"the girl who tried to commit suicide."

But there was more than embarrassment to deal with the next day when the head of the unit came in to report the results of the tests. He explained that my kyphosis was a clear indication that the initial operations performed at Mercy hadn't been successful. And the long hours I'd been expected to sit up hadn't helped matters any either.

I listened, unsure where he was going until he said, "I see two options for you. You can wear a body brace for an indefinite period of time, or we can redo the surgery. My personal recommendation, however, because of the success rate, is surgery."

All the anticipation I'd felt in coming to Philadelphia was snuffed out in that moment. All I could think of was the past three months of suffering, and I knew I couldn't go through it again.

Mom was silent. I didn't look over at her because I didn't want her to read the panic in my eyes.

Chapter 22

The doctor explained that the recovery from this repeat surgery would be much quicker—partly because I was stronger now, but also because of the advanced procedures in use at Jefferson. I remembered the terrible struggle I'd had with breathing and the times I thought I'd choke to death on the congestion in my chest. But when the doctor learned how some of the hospital personnel back in Wilkes-Barre had demanded I try to cough to break up the congestion, he was incredulous. "It's physically impossible for a person with your kind of paralysis to cough like that." And he assured me that such measures would not be used; the entire staff at Jefferson was so experienced in spinal cord injuries that my recovery from surgery should proceed without any more hitches.

As he went on to explain the details of my coming treatment, the doubts and dread began to mount. He told me that, after the surgery, I'd be placed in halo-femural traction to keep my back as straight as possible, rendering my body completely immobile.

"How does it work?" I asked.

"It's really nothing more than a fancy brace. The halo is actually a stainless steel band that encircles the head and is attached to the skull with a couple screws to hold it rigid."

My expression must have registered my alarm because he hastened on. "The screws are only inserted a little way into the skull. You'll be given an anesthetic and the process shouldn't be painful."

My mind tried to deny what I was hearing. "Two more pins will be inserted in your legs, into the femur actually, just above the knees. You probably won't be able to feel those at all. And then we'll attach wires and weights to the halo and the femural pins to provide the traction, which will help prevent the recurrence of kyphosis.

"You'll only be confined to bed for a couple weeks after the surgery. Then we'll gradually get you up. Even with the halo, you'll be tooling around in a wheelchair in no time.

"The bed you'll have in the meantime is a special one called a Roto Rest Kinetic Treatment Table. It's especially designed for patients who have to be immobilized for a period of time. It rotates to prevent bedsores."

"What do you mean, 'it rotates'?" I pictured an absurd contraption—sort of a cross between a hospital bed and a cheap whirling carnival ride.

"It turns slowly from one side to the other, about 45 degrees or so to keep the blood flowing and avoid skin breakdown. But it moves so slowly you won't even feel the movement. Don't worry, we never have any complaints about it."

In Philadelphia, the order of the two surgeries was reversed. The anterior laminectomy came first, on May 13; the posterior laminectomy was performed on May 28. Mary woke up on May 29 in the intensive care unit.

Consciousness returned slowly. First there were noises. The soft whirring of machines. Voices, faint and distant, then closer. And there was the pain—gripping, shooting, searing pain that came from everywhere at once, but especially from my back. Trying to orient myself, I opened my eyes.

What I saw made no sense. I waited for my eyes to adjust to the light and my vision to clear. What I saw above me looked like a floor. The surface glistened as if freshly polished. There were squares in the pattern about the size of floor tiles . . . they *were* floor tiles. *Then that's the floor. I'm looking down, not up. And . . .* With the realization that I was suspended upside down, I interrupted my own thoughts with a cry for help.

I heard someone hurrying toward me. "Are you awake now, Mary?" A pair of white nurse's shoes came into view.

"Am I on a Stryker frame?" I gasped out the words.

"Yes, you are. But only until—"

I didn't wait to hear how long I was doomed to this agony. I struggled against the restraints, recalling a movie I'd seen during junior and senior high-school days. For me, the most horrible part of *The Other Side of the Mountain*—a true story about a downhill skier paralyzed in an accident—was her confinement in a Stryker frame where she remained hour after hour, unable to see anything but the floor.

Finally the nurse succeeded in calming me. Assuring me that the Stryker was only temporary, she explained it was merely a means to keep my back immobilized until they could get my halo rigged up in a day or so and fit me for a body vest.

I hoped she was telling me the truth. But I wasn't sure. After all, no one had warned me about the Stryker.

The nurse was right though. The next day an orthopedic specialist came to my room to "install" the halo. First, he gave me an injection in my head—a local anesthetic. After waiting a short time for the medicine to take effect, he took out a stainless steel band that I recognized immediately as the halo—two very long stainless steel screws and what looked like an ordinary Phillips-head screwdriver. While I lay there, fully awake, he put the halo in place and began screwing those big screws right into my skull. While the anesthetic may have dulled the sharpest pain, I still felt an excruciating pressure as I heard the sickening sound of metal twisting into bone.

The resulting headache didn't ease up for several days. My head felt like it was clamped in a vise that was only gradually loosened.

Once I was in bed, wired to the weights that pulled both at

my head and my legs, I wasn't going anywhere. The complete setup looked and felt like some high-tech version of a medieval torture rack—a sort of horizontal crucifixion.

This new ordeal became a test of my young faith, my new relationship with God. As each boring, exhausting, uncomfortable day passed, I found renewed strength. During the long, dreary hours on the roto-bed, my mother read to me from Joni Eareckson's books, *Joni* and *A Step Further*. This remarkable young quadriplegic's moving story of learning to accept her fate as a blessing rather than a curse gave me inspiration and hope. We bought tapes of Joni's music and listened to them again and again. Especially meaningful to me was her song about her wheelchair and how God had set her mind and spirit free.

My mother read to me from the Bible too, and I listened to inspiring Christian music by such performers as Keith Green and Amy Grant. So even though a total of five weeks in a constantly moving bed and two more major surgeries reduced my body to skin and bones, I felt my faith growing stronger.

Despite the progress I was making in some areas, I still struggled with my attitude toward food. One day, shortly after my second surgery, a nurse came in for my menu selection for dinner. "I'll just have the salad with your diet dressing, please," I told her.

"No way, young lady!" she snapped back. "You need to build yourself up. You need as many calories as you can get."

That incident made me realize again the depths of my eating problem. And I wondered if I'd ever have a normal attitude toward food again.

My greatest hope for complete emotional recovery came to rest in the counseling of Dr. Richard Fitzgibbons, a Philadelphia psychiatrist to whom I had been referred by a friend. He didn't visit me at Jefferson, but we talked on the phone every few days.

Gently but firmly, he urged me to face and talk about the feelings I had toward others and toward myself. He helped me recognize my anger, my frustrations, and my fear. One day he suggested I pray, forgiving anyone toward whom I might be harboring any resentment—my family, for holding the kind of expectations that made me such a high achiever; my friends, for not knowing how to help me before it was too late; the doctors, for inflicting such unpleasant treatment on me; even myself, for trying to take my own life. So I prayed, right there on the phone, and felt a weight of bitterness I hadn't even known existed, lift off.

Another time, as I talked about the pain I was having to endure, Dr. Fitzgibbons suggested I offer my suffering to God on behalf of others. To think of it not just as my own personal pain, but as an act of sacrifice and service I could make for others. And when I did that, I found fresh endurance that brought more relief than any medication.

We continued to talk, and I found it easy to be as honest with Dr. Fitzgibbons as I was with my sister Judy. Once, when I was confessing feelings of frustration and discouragement, he gave me a unique idea. He said, "Try to imagine—actually picture in your mind—Christ standing beside you, or sitting with you, offering his strength and comfort."

After that, on nights when I couldn't sleep, I imagined myself being held and rocked in the arms of Jesus until the peace of sleep washed over me.

Though I had yet to meet the psychiatrist face to face, he was more helpful than all the other counselors, all the mental wards, all the group therapy I'd had in the previous nine months. Not only did he know and practice his discipline of psychiatry, but he understood that true emotional and mental healing also requires spiritual healing. I could sense his caring, his compassion, as we talked on the phone. And we never ended a conversation without one or both of us praying about the matters we'd just discussed. So he also taught me the therapeutic value of prayer.

Physical progress came much more slowly. A little more than a week after the second surgery, after weeks of lying in a horizontal position, the head of my bed was elevated by 15 degrees. I felt as if I was going to topple over. But my equilibrium gradually returned, and the next day the nurse increased the angle to 30 degrees; then 45 and 60. Each time, the new height made me dizzy until my body adjusted to the changes. But the steady progress was exhilarating.

Exhilaration gave way to exhaustion the day I was placed in a reclining wheelchair and instructed to wheel myself to the end of the hall and back. Thirty feet felt like a marathon.

And each day I was expected to accomplish more. After only a few days of physical therapy in my room, I was deemed strong enough to go to the PT gym to work on rebuilding my muscle tone and to learn some essential skills—how to keep my balance when sitting up, and how to transfer from bed to wheelchair, or vice versa.

In PT, I gained more than physical strength and skill. I made a whole new set of friends—others who were also struggling with handicaps, some far worse than mine. One woman had MS, and there were a couple elderly people who had been robbed and beaten. One young man, the victim of a rugby accident, had sustained an injury that required him to be on a respirator for the rest of his life. A marketing specialist was now brain-damaged from a gang beating. And as I got to know these people, as I watched them coping courageously, as I understood their handicaps, I began to count my blessings—sight, speech, the use of my hands, my mind.

My mother's pastor, Dr. Jule Ayers, came to visit one day. As we talked about my daily struggles and emotional highs and lows, he proposed that I pick one word each week—love, peace, joy—qualities that should characterize a Christian's life. Then he challenged me to look for examples in my daily life and in the lives of people around me.

I accepted the challenge. The first word I chose was *victory.* Each day of the next week, I measured my success in millimeters. My nausea left. I was able to eat a chocolate bar a visitor left me. I wheeled myself down the hall. Small celebrations to some, perhaps, but to me they represented important milestones.

Finally, after being confined inside hospital walls for nearly five months and suffering the darkness of my bulimia and anorexia for almost a year before that, I was strong enough to get my first pass and be wheeled outside. Father's Day 1982 was a landmark day for me. I saw the light of a new world through new eyes. The sun became God's warmth soaking though my entire being. I was a new person. I felt free and alive again, more alive than I'd ever been in my entire life.

I ate an ice cream cone. And it tasted good.

Chapter 23

Over the following days and weeks, I used my passes to get out as often as possible, savoring the delicious sensation of newfound happiness.

I specifically recall the evening of the Fourth of July. Mom, Dad, and I went to a Chinese restaurant to celebrate the holiday. Afterwards we went back to the hospital, where we joined a number of mobile patients on an observation deck on the top floor. There, with a crowd of patients and staff, we watched the fireworks display over Veteran's Stadium. A jovial black nurse with a marvelous voice belted out a powerful rendition of the "Star Spangled Banner" as the rockets' red, white, and blue glare burst across Philadelphia's night sky. And when the show finally concluded, someone brought out a guitar and led us all in a rousing group sing.

As I sang that night and felt my emotions soar with the music, I couldn't help thinking back over the year before. While my physical paralysis seemed a terrible ordeal, the emotional paralysis I'd endured for so many months had been far worse. I'd felt dead—lost to myself. But now God had given me back my feelings. I was finding myself again. I was learning how to live.

A big step in my learning process came just a couple days later on July 6 when I was released from Jefferson and transferred to Magee Rehabilitation Center just a few blocks away. At Magee I was forced to face my limitations and challenged to use all my strength to master the survival skills required for a lifetime as a paraplegic.

Physical therapy proved to be a test of endurance. Every morning after breakfast I'd go to the gym and work out until noon. Weight training strengthened the arm muscles that had grown weak with months of little use. I did push-ups by the dozens—regular ones lying on my stomach and then sitting push-ups, using the arms of my chair to hoist my whole body off the seat.

My history of tough athletic training helped a lot. I'd never shied away from physical exertion or pain in pursuit of my goals. So despite the frustration of my new limitations, it felt good, familiar really, to be challenged physically, to work hard.

All in all, I had an incredibly busy summer. Every weekend I'd go out with my parents to some museum or historical site. And I'd use nearly every visit from friends as an excuse to get out of the hospital to catch a movie, eat at some restaurant, or just take in some of the sights. In addition to all my visitors, I had a steady stream of cards, letters, and calls from friends back home and from running friends I'd made around the country. And their attention and concern, as well as the constant devotion of my family, made me feel a greater sense of love and acceptance than I'd ever known before.

One of the most moving gestures of all came on July 18 when the Wyoming Valley Striders, my local running club, sponsored the "Mary Wazeter Benefit Run" in Wilkes-Barre. The mayor declared a "Mary Wazeter Week," and my home church sponsored an ice cream social to help raise additional funds.

The race itself turned out to be quite an extravaganza. Marathon champion Bill Rogers, who'd stood on the victory stand in New York with me when we won the Pepsi 10K race, sent his personal greetings to be read to all the entrants. My Warren Street friends ran, as did my Georgetown team, a team from Franklin and Marshall, and over 800 others. The result was the largest roadrace ever held in that part of the country and a fund-raising event that provided several thousand dollars to help defray the enormous medical bills my family and I faced as a result of my ordeal.

But as much as the money meant to me, what mattered even more was what this effort symbolized. I'd always valued the running friendships I'd developed over the years, and one of the biggest fears I faced in the wake of my injuries was losing those friends forever. The race convinced me I was wrong. I still had my friends, more than I'd ever guessed. And their support challenged me to work even harder at my rehabilitation.

One day, not long after I'd transferred to Magee, a man I'd never seen before walked into my room. A handsome, silver-haired gentleman, he was slight of build and walked with a noticeable limp. He smiled kindly as he approached and asked, "Do you know who I am?"

"The voice is familiar, but I don't . . ." I tried to place him. Suddenly I knew. "You're Dr. Fitzgibbons!"

"Yes, I am." His blue eyes twinkled warmly as he laughed and gently took my hand.

We talked for a long time that day. He told me that he had been a counselor for years but had been frustrated with the inability of psychiatry to help so many of his patients. Then he'd personally committed his own life to living for Christ and began looking for ways to incorporate spiritual faith into the emotional and mental healing of his clients. Now, he said, there were far more rewards than frustrations in his work.

I was greatly encouraged when he said, "I can see a growing strength in you already, Mary."

Proof of his words was my lack of concern about what other people thought about me, or how I looked to others. The painful self-consciousness I'd felt about my appearance for so many years slowly disappeared that summer. I went all over Philadelphia in a wheelchair with a body brace that made me look more like a space creature than a human being, but I learned to smile and accept the stares. I realized I couldn't live any kind of active, rewarding life if I went around worrying about what other people were thinking about me.

One day the Carrol twins—two sisters who had run with me in junior and senior high—dropped by to visit. They were pushing me along the sidewalk several blocks from the hospital when one of the wheels on my wheelchair broke. Each of them grabbed an arm of my chair and carried me back to the hospital, laughing all the way. My reaction caused me to realize I was no longer a prisoner to the thoughts and opinions of others.

This discovery was reinforced when Bob made his first visit to Philadelphia to see me. I put on makeup for the first time in ages and tried to look nice—as nice as I could look, sitting in a wheelchair with my sci-fi contraption only partially covered by a shirt twice my usual size. I hadn't seen him in months and I wanted things to go well.

We ate lunch together in the atrium cafeteria. He told me about his year at school and about his summer job. I told him about my hospital routine. When one of my doctors walked by, I waved, feeling proud to be seen with Bobby. In that sense it seemed natural to be with him again. But it also felt a little awkward, strained. While we had never officially broken up, our old relationship had pretty much ended during the summer before I went off to college. We'd drifted apart and we both knew it. It would have been silly to pretend otherwise.

I still cared deeply about him. But as much as I might have liked to recapture the feelings we once had, I knew we couldn't. Not so much because of my physical condition, but because we were now two very different people, going in different directions. And I wanted to say all that, to let him know how I felt . . . When the time was right.

"Want to catch a movie?" he asked after lunch. "I'll bet *E.T.* is showing somewhere nearby."

I hadn't seen the year's big blockbuster movie, so I was game. "Sure," I agreed. "Let's get a paper and find out where."

It was playing at a movie house only a few blocks away. I thought I knew right where the theater was, so we got a pass and Bob wheeled me out of the hospital and down the street. But by the time we'd gone three or four blocks, we realized we weren't going to make the one o'clock show.

As we reached the park across the street from Independence Hall, I said, "Why don't we stop here and talk for a while?"

So that's where I said my piece. I told Bob I didn't want him to think that what had happened between us had anything to do with our relationship. Or with him. I didn't want him blaming himself. I didn't blame him. My problems dated back to patterns and personality traits developed in childhood, long before I met Bobby.

I told him about the most recent changes. I told him I knew I was a new person now and that God would be with me through whatever lay ahead. While I didn't come right out and say I didn't want him to feel obligated to me, I wanted him to know it. So I told him I knew we'd been growing apart for a long time and that I didn't think it would be possible to pick up where we'd left off, though I hoped we could continue to be friends.

It wasn't easy opening up like that. Bob didn't say much, but I could tell he was relieved I'd spoken up. And he assured me he wanted our friendship to continue too.

"If we hurry, we can catch the three o'clock showing," he said, after what seemed like an eternity of talking.

We laughed and cheered E.T. with everyone else in the movie audience. And then it was back to the hospital for our good-byes. We made no plans. Only promises to stay in touch. And he was gone. With him went a part of me. And that felt sad. But as he left, I felt a sense of letting go. And that felt right.

The staff at Magee kept preaching the importance of independence. They encouraged my mom to go home for a couple weeks; so after months of being with me every day and living out of a suitcase, she went back to Wilkes-Barre. And I was on my own, without the emotional support of her presence for the first time since the bridge. During the two weeks Mom was home, I discovered new reserves of personal strength and an added appreciation for the sacrificial support my family had been giving me.

August 18, the day I'd been both looking forward to and dreading all summer, finally came. This was the day the halo was to come off. And while I could hardly wait, I still had a horribly vivid image of the doctor with the Phillips-head screwdriver, turning those big screws into my skull.

But the reverse procedure proved relatively painless. Two technicians, looking like a couple well-scrubbed mechanics, showed up with a toolbox. I tensed up, afraid that when they removed the halo supporting my head, it would loll to the side like that of a well-worn rag doll. But the technicians assured me that they would fit me with a collar to take the place of my atrophied neck muscles until they could do their job again.

My scalp bled a bit when they took out the screws. But a tourniquet on my head soon took care of the bleeding and made me resemble the picture on the front cover of *The Red Badge of Courage.*

In September, the staff at Magee sent me home for four weeks. The idea was partly to get a short respite from six months of hospitalization. But this was also an excellent opportunity to get a taste of life on the outside, so I'd know what skills I needed to perfect. In the bargain, it was a chance for my family to make a more realistic assessment of what life would be like when I came home for good.

It wasn't easy. The house wasn't exactly designed for someone with my handicap. Yet it was the house I'd grown up in, a house full of warm, wonderful memories. And unlike the last few visits, this time it felt like home again. When a few friends showed up to celebrate my nineteenth birthday, I felt none of the awkwardness or embarrassment I'd felt about my emotional problems the previous Christmas.

At the suggestion of Dr. Fitzgibbons, I signed up for a weekend retreat sponsored by the Philadelphia Chapter of the HEC (Handicapped Encounter Christ). What I experienced at that retreat moved and inspired me. I particularly remember one man who was so severely deformed that he'd spent his entire life—thirty-five years—lying on a prone cart. He couldn't feed, bathe, or dress himself. He was completely helpless, completely dependent on others. And yet I saw joy all over his face as he joined the group in singing songs of praise to God.

The joy must have been contagious, because during the retreat a girl with cerebral palsy approached me and asked, "How can you be so happy?" I had to confess that I wasn't always happy and told her about my struggle with depression. She wept as she confessed a similar battle. As I listened, I realized how far I'd come. And I tried to explain to her the help I'd found in my relationship with God.

I came home from that weekend, realizing that if people like the man on that prone cart could find happiness, I could too. And after my talk with the girl who had CP, I decided that I wanted to help others find the peace I'd found. Then maybe, just maybe, I could be the inspiration to others my mother had told me I could be.

On October 11, I returned to Magee for the final phase of my rehabilitation program. I was discharged, at last, on December 17, 1982, and returned to Wilkes-Barre in time for Christmas with my family.

Chapter 24

I returned to Magee for a couple more months of rehabilitation training. Then it was back to Wilkes-Barre for good.

It felt great to be home. But I soon grew restless—to do something, to feel useful. So I signed on to work as a volunteer with a local inner-city mission to the poor and homeless. My first assignment was tutoring a forty-year-old man who wanted to learn to read and write. I discovered that helping someone else was the quickest way to take my mind off my own problems.

By the time winter melted away, I felt strong enough to sign up for one class—a psychology course—at Wilkes-Barre's own King's College. I received regular physical therapy at a local rehab center and in April I learned to swim as a paraplegic.

The doctors at Thomas Jefferson had told me I'd never be able to swim again, but Bob Bergstrasser, the athletic trainer at King's College, worked with me until I felt confident enough to swim alone. Daily workouts in the pool did more to put me back in shape than any exercise I'd been doing for over a year. I was on the road back to good health—if not to wholeness.

I experienced a small setback in May of 1983 when my doctor diagnosed a potentially worsening case of scoliosis or curvature of the spine and recommended yet another operation. The procedure called for two stainless steel Luque rods, fourteen inches long and three-eights of an inch in diameter, to be inserted on either side of my spinal column to keep it straight.

I went back to Philadelphia, this time to the Children's Hospital, for surgery on the sixth of May. Less than three weeks later, on May 25, I enrolled in two classes for King's summer term.

By the end of summer school I'd worked myself up to a pretty strenuous daily routine. I'd wheel myself one and a half miles to school in the morning for my ten o'clock class. When I got out at noon I'd spend forty-five minutes swimming laps in the college pool before Dad or the public transportation van would pick me up and take me home for an afternoon of studying. After supper Dad would drive me back to the campus for my evening class.

That fall I took a full college load—five courses. I kept up my daily swimming routine and managed to pull down a 3.5 average for the term. I started an eating disorder group on campus under the guidance of the school counselor and planned to major in psychology, with hopes that someday I'd be able to counsel others suffering emotionally and physically.

My feelings about my own physical condition plummeted in November when one of the Luque rods in my back caused a large cyst to protrude from my back. The doctor recommended another surgery, this time to shorten the rods and reduce the irritation.

While recovering from this latest surgery, my hopes went soaring one day in December.

Sitting on my bed that morning, the thought struck me, *Try to move your toes.* From time to time since my injuries, well-meaning friends and relatives had said to me, "Just concentrate and try to move your toes, Mary." I had always tried, with no success. But this time an inner voice was speaking, so I tried once again. My big toe flexed the tiniest bit. At least I thought it moved. *Maybe my eyes are playing tricks.* I tried again. Once more I saw a flicker of movement. I was so sure of it that I called to my parents. Again the toe twitched—ever so slightly. Their excitement fueled mine, and for a moment we allowed ourselves a moment of hilarity.

Next time I saw my doctor, I showed him the movement and asked what it meant. He admitted that since my spinal cord had never been severed, there was always a chance I could regain movement. But his words were guarded and he urged me not to get my hopes up.

A miracle hardly seemed out of the question. So many unbelievable things had already happened in two years since I'd jumped off the bridge.

I'd seen my story impact more people than I ever imagined I could reach. In April of 1983, Neal Amdur, a sports writer for the *New York Times* wrote up my ordeal with anorexia in a story that made the front page of the Sunday sports section. *Seventeen* magazine did a short story that summer, *People* magazine did a photo feature, and *Young Miss* published the account I'd written myself when I was still in the hospital.

I was interviewed by Jane Pauley on NBC's "Today" show and appeared on Pat Robertson's "700 Club" to warn others about the threat of anorexia and talk about the healing strength I'd found in my faith. In the spring of 1984 *Campus Life* magazine published the most complete account of my ordeal to date in a long, two-part story.

But what was most exciting about the chance to share my story through the media wasn't merely the fact that I was reaching millions of people, but the response that came in the wake of the publicity—personal letters, phone calls, and visits. I began to correspond and talk with numerous girls from around the country suffering from anorexia or bulimia and developed an ongoing relationship with some of them, sharing my own faith and encouraging them in their personal battles.

Various publishers began contacting me with regard to writing a book about my experiences—a book that would encourage even more people. The idea became more and more appealing.

So with all these good things already happening, it didn't seem unreasonable to hope for a miracle: Maybe, just maybe I *would* walk again. What a powerful witness that would be if I could stand up and tell everyone: "God has healed me!" What a great ending for a book! What a wonderful finish for my long marathon journey out of personal despair!

While I couldn't yet see the finish line, I felt certain the worst of my course was behind me now, and the going would all be downhill from here on. But I was wrong.

Chapter 25

No further physical progress occurred in the next few months. And when change did come in the spring of 1984, it was for the worse.

I began experiencing such terrible pain from sitting that I had to lie down between classes. I had to write so many papers, propped up on my arms, that the skin on my elbows began to break down into painful sores. I finished the term, but I decided to skip summer school in hopes the doctors could do something for, or at least explain the cause of the excruciating pain in my lower body when I had to sit up—even for short periods of time.

The next couple years took me on a discouraging, fruitless search from doctor to doctor, trying to find some relief or explanation. One doctor offered the disheartening word that he'd seen some patients who weren't able to cope without becoming addicted to pain-killing drugs. Having to reduce my school load was also discouraging. But the people at King's were most cooperative; they allowed me to have a cot in my classroom when I could no longer bear to sit up, and my professors permitted me to do verbal term papers and take verbal tests. I managed to tolerate this torture for three consecutive terms at King's. But finally in February of 1986 I reached a point where concentration became impossible. And I once again dropped out of college.

At this physical and emotional low point, I did receive, at last, a word of encouragement regarding my continuous pain. A neurologist who came to visit me said he thought the pain I was experiencing was a result of my nerves slowly regenerating. And the best word of all was this: instead of predicting I'd have the pain the rest of my life, he said he thought it would recede slowly over the next year. I prayed he was right. And I began to believe it.

Sure enough, in May of 1986, the agonizing pain began to dissipate. Within a few weeks it was entirely gone. I wasn't any closer to walking, but after spending most of two years lying in bed, sitting up again seemed like no small miracle. Now I could really get on with my life!

For so many months Mary had lived in a confined, controlled environment. Expectations had been limited by the pain that precluded attending school, let alone setting life goals. Suddenly, almost overnight, the horizons of her world were shoved back. Whereas before, almost all Mary's energy had been spent in enduring the pain and difficulties of day-to-day existence, now she had the resources to consider her future again.

With her book manuscript finished, Mary now hoped to be physically strong enough to do interviews and promotion when the book was published the next year. She began to dream big about the impact this book could have and the number of people she'd be able to help.

In the fall she could go back to school to resume work toward a degree in psychology. This training would enable her to counsel others who were going through the nightmare she had endured.

She could also begin thinking more about long-term goals of independent living. While in constant pain, she had been able to do so little for herself that it had been impossible to imagine living on her own. Now the thought of moving out of her parents' home and establishing a life of her own not only seemed possible, it appeared to be a very necessary step in her pursuit of a satisfying, well-adjusted life.

Suddenly there seemed so much to be done that I was almost overwhelmed by my options. To prepare myself for the challenges ahead, I devoted the summer to a regimen of physical and spiritual training. I was up and out of the house by six each morning to wheel myself three miles through downtown Wilkes-Barre and over a bridge to Kirby Park and then back home around nine. Many evenings I'd go out wheeling again. In the time between workouts, I spent hours reading my Bible in search of encouragement and direction for my life.

Mary needed reassurance because the very same possibilities that excited her about the future also promised changes and challenges. And that worried her. Was she ready for the pressures she'd have to face?

She tried to put up a positive front. She testified how God had healed her from her pain and that she felt good about the future. But her determinedly upbeat attitude masked hidden fears. And the more she denied her anxieties, the harder it became to admit them—even to herself. Her rigorous training routine and her Bible study intensified to the point of obsession as the summer wore on. But even that couldn't push the anxiety out of her mind for long.

I'd be wheeling hard along a deserted city street at six in the morning, with my mind clear of everything but the sense of exertion—that old-friend feeling of protesting muscles pushed to their limits and the accompanying sounds of my own pounding heart and heavy rhythmic breathing. The familiar sensations reassured me: *I'm still alive and everything is going to be okay.*

Then I'd hear a car approaching from behind and my mind would freeze. All the nerves in my body would contract and I'd feel a flash of terrifying uncertainty until the car passed and was out of sight. It was the same kind of confused, panicky feeling I'd gotten at Georgetown when I'd be running alone on those Washington D.C. streets.

After all I'd been through since I'd left for Georgetown five years before, after all the progress I thought I'd made, after all the people I'd told about God's help and healing, after everything—that same helpless, out-of-control feeling was back. *Something is still wrong with me!* I couldn't deny it to myself any longer. But I couldn't bring myself to admit it to anyone else either. I merely devoted more and more time to training and Bible reading.

Concerned about her increasingly obsessive exercise and Bible reading, Mary's parents called in Dr. Fitzgibbons for counseling once a week. His diagnosis proved accurate: Mary was suffering from acute anxiety and depression.

After two years of being limited and controlled by pain, the "unlimited" feel of her life provided many understandable reasons for Mary's anxiety. Schoolwork had always meant pressure. Would she be able to handle a full academic load? Or did those panicky feelings mean she was headed for another nightmare experience like the one at Georgetown?

How would she fit in socially? All the friends she'd started college with had graduated by now. Going back to school meant she'd have to make all new acquaintances again. Would people accept her?

What about the future? Now that pain no longer stood in her way, Mary felt she had to make plans and begin working toward a more independent life. Could she really do that? Could she ever live on her own?

And then there was the pending lawsuit. Mary and her parents had been reluctant to take legal action after Mary was injured. Yet it seemed quite clear to the Wazeters' advisors that the hospital and the psychiatrist, who had released Mary with the assurance that she was no longer suicidal the day before she jumped off the bridge, had been negligent and were at least partly responsible for what happened. A settlement would not only help with the medical bills, but would provide Mary with the added resources she'd need to live independently after her parents were gone. At long last, the court date was set for September of 1986, but required long hours of deposition, testimony, and painful memories to be relived and retold throughout that summer.

Having to see Dr. Fitzgibbons on a weekly basis seemed like a giant step backward for Mary, just when she thought she was ready to move ahead. The mini-panic attacks greatly troubled her. And when Dr. Fitzgibbons recommended she give herself more time to make adjustments and wait until January to go back to school, Mary found his "cure" to be even more depressing. The prospect of sitting out yet another semester of classes made her feel lazy, worthless, and purposeless. The deepening depression multiplied the stress and anxiety which resulted in more depression; Mary's life was spinning in a vicious downward cycle until she finally succumbed to the same pattern of response to stress that she had adopted back at Georgetown. Mary began to binge.

It began at home with things I didn't think my parents would notice—a box of crackers here, a half-dozen slices of bread there. But my preoccupation with eating quickly progressed to junk food again. I'd tell my parents I was going uptown to swim, but instead I'd take a few dollars and buy candy and cookies to gorge on.

The lawsuit was finally settled just before we went to court. But even that occurrence and the possibility it provided for an independent future, did little or nothing to relieve my growing sense of despair.

I remember one particular day when I'd spent all my cash and still wanted more to eat. I was about to head for home and see what I could scrounge up there, when I saw an old bag lady sitting on a park bench. I didn't know her name, but she often wandered the streets of downtown Wilkes-Barre, wearing a ratty old wedding dress and muttering incoherently to herself. Rumor had it she'd been stood up by her fiance on her wedding day and hadn't been right since. So I rolled my chair over to this pathetic woman's seat, smiled my best smile, and interrupted her unintelligible monologue to ask: "Do you have any money? I'm hungry."

She studied me for a few moments with glazed eyes. Then she

glanced down at my wheelchair and a look of sad kindness transformed her face. She smiled at me as she reached into her dress. "Here ya go, honey," she said, pulling out two dollar bills.

I thanked her and hurriedly rolled away down the street. But I'd no sooner wolfed down another two dollars worth of junk food than I felt doubly sick. Sick from my bloated stomach, yes. But even more sick with guilt.

I'd already completed a book manuscript about my experience, that was at that moment sitting in a publisher's office waiting to be edited and then published sometime in the coming year. The whole purpose of the book was to inspire and encourage others, to let them know that with God's help they could overcome their problems, just as I'd overcome my anorexia and bulimia.

Now suddenly I felt like such a hypocrite. The book seemed a cruel hoax. Not only had I failed to overcome my eating disorder, I'd actually fallen to a new low. I was shamelessly begging binge money from mentally disturbed street people!

Not long after that I was invited to a wedding where I bumped into an old high-school friend, Lisa Richards. I spared her the goriest, most embarrassing details of the last few years, but for three hours I poured out my feelings of despair. She called my parents a little later and told them she was sure I could get the help I needed in the unit of the hospital where she worked in Philadelphia. And while I had lost all faith in hospitals, I agreed to go. The only other option I could see was dying.

The structured, behavioristic routine of the hospital enabled me to stop binging almost immediately. I even became something of a celebrity in the unit when the ABC Sunday evening news ran an interview I'd done some months earlier with Edie Magnus as part of a feature on eating disorders and athletes. But every morning I awakened in that hospital was a depressing reminder that I was worse off than I'd been in that first psych unit at Georgetown five years before—this time I was in a psych unit in a *wheelchair*.

With my binging back under control, the focus of my treatment at the hospital was to plan toward independence. The staff seemed to feel I could overcome my depression with the sense of accomplishment and satisfaction that would come as I left home and struck out on my own. Since nothing else had worked, I quickly bought into their thinking.

When I was released and went home a few weeks before Christmas, plans were well underway. My sister Judy and her husband, Bill, were all for the idea. Judy began looking for a wheelchair-accessible apartment near her home in Virginia Beach, Virginia. Once she found a place, I'd move down there, hire an aide to live with me, and then begin school at Virginia Wesleyan. Judy was so optimistic about the prospects that my own hopes began to rise. Maybe we could make this work. Maybe all I really needed was a chance to prove to myself that I could make it on my own. Achieving independence would be a great way to end the book, which had been temporarily put on hold.

Over Christmas, the temptation to binge on all the holiday goodies around the house unsettled me; I wondered if I really would be able to handle living on my own. But I maintained control and actually began to lose the extra pounds I'd put on during the months of overeating.

Finding a manageable apartment in Virginia Beach proved harder than we'd imagined. I finally enrolled in the county community college in Wilkes-Barre while I waited for Judy to work out the details on her end. And I kept the urge to binge under control by mostly avoiding food.

In fact, my weight continued to drop. One morning I wheeled into the kitchen where my father was fixing his breakfast. "Dad," I began hesitantly, "I think I have anorexia again."

He sighed and looked at me sadly. "I'm glad you're admitting it, at least," he said. "That's the first step."

The problem was that none of us knew what second step to take. We'd tried everything before.

My weight peeled away until I was at my all-time low of 85

pounds again. Just as at Georgetown, the resulting chemical imbalance made it impossible for me to concentrate enough to do my schoolwork. When I began to hallucinate and refused to eat, drink, or talk, my parents felt they had no choice but to commit me to a hospital outside Philadelphia. From there I was transferred to yet another hospital in Philly; by that time I was binging again. The only way the staff could control me at all was to pump me full of medication and physically restrain me.

In a last-ditch measure, Judy found a hospital with an eating disorder unit near her home in Norfolk, Virginia. In desperation, knowing that none of the other hospitals had helped, my parents agreed to yet another transfer.

For the first time, I was in a hospital with other young women who had the same eating disorder I had. Seeing those skeletal frames walking up and down the hallway, I thought: *These girls are where I was five years ago. If I could only have found a place like this back then, maybe things could have been different. But it's too late now. There's no more hope.*

I refused to cooperate with the program and even escaped from the hospital once in a desperate search for a vending machine. One of the doctors told my family he thought I might have to be hospitalized for the rest of my life. I was so obviously the worst case in the unit that I became a staff scare-tactic to be used on the other patients. "If you don't make some changes," girls were told, "you could end up like Mary."

But I finally signed a written contract to abide by the rules of the program. Not because I thought the program would work for me. But because I knew there was no other way to get out. I couldn't exist in a hospital for the rest of my life. And if death was the only solution (which now seemed more and more likely), I couldn't very easily commit suicide in a hospital either. So the only option was to cooperate. Again, cooperation paid off.

Shortly after my release, Judy located an ideal apartment. So with no better plan in mind, my parents reluctantly agreed to let me move to Virginia Beach. Judy arranged for a live-in aide,

Beth, a student at CBN University; Judy also set me up with a Christian counselor.

But the very first day, when the aide left me alone to go to class, I binged. And the pattern continued all summer. She knew it. Judy knew it. When they asked me about it, I admitted it. They'd have known soon anyway because I began to balloon—gaining over twenty pounds in two months. When Beth moved everything sweet out of reach, I was left with whatever food I could find in the refrigerator—sometimes consuming whole sticks of margarine and cleaning out peanut butter jars by the tablespoonful.

By the end of the summer, even Mary's ever-faithful, optimistic sister Judy was nearing the end of her patience. So when Mary's roommate Beth announced her engagement and decided to move back to her hometown, the Wazeter family faced a serious crisis. Mary had been so out of control with an aide, there was no way they could trust her to live by herself—even for a few days. So while a search was begun to find another live-in companion, Mary entered yet another hospital. This time it was a brand-new psych unit attached to a local hospital, but managed and run by Christians with the goal of treating patients spiritually as well as emotionally and physically. "Maybe this is just the kind of help you need," Judy encouraged her sister.

Mary wasn't convinced. Desperately needing some sense of forward movement in her life, she argued and screamed and begged the hospital staff to make an exception and give her a day pass so she could begin the fall term at Virginia Wesleyan. College, even the one course she planned to take—a human resources course called "Introduction to Human Service"—represented progress, or at least the hope of progress.

The hospital staff finally consented. And Mary began commuting from the hospital to her classes on the Virginia Wesleyan campus. A little more than a month into the term Judy found another CBN student willing to live with Mary and the hospital released her to go home—not because she'd made significant progress in therapy, but because it was a short-term unit and Mary had overstayed their time limits.

Mary's new roommate, Nan, kept an even closer watch on her at the apartment. So Mary began doing most of her serious binging at school where the vending machines proved a stronger attraction than the lectures. Some days she didn't even bother going to class. She'd just head for the student union building, drop four or five dollars worth of change into the vending machines, and then find a private place where she'd stuff herself with her hoard of candy and cookies.

One day when her dad was down for a visit, he drove to the campus to pick Mary up after class. He located the right room, but when class was dismissed, Mary didn't come out. He inquired of the professor who said Mary had been absent. Alarmed at that report, he hurriedly scouted the small campus, asking students and faculty if they'd seen "the girl in the wheelchair." She'd last been seen at the student center; so he focused his search in that building. That's where he finally found Mary, sitting in a locked bathroom stall, cramming candy bars and cookies into her mouth with two hands. And as he drove his daughter back to her apartment, Leon Wazeter wept in helpless despair.

Once again I was numb to my father's pain. One day that fall I wrote this description of my feelings:

"Everywhere life is going on around me. People are smiling, crying, laughing. But I feel dead. I'm a walking zombie with no emotions. So where do I go? Whom do I turn to? I've learned it's not where I am that matters, it's who I am. And I detest the girl who peeks back at me in the mirror."

That girl looked fat. Before, though I'd been in a wheelchair and my body no longer worked, I'd consoled myself with the thought that at least I *looked* like a runner. Now, losing that small consolation felt like the final blow.

Dying was again the only hope I could see for ending my misery. "But," I wrote in my journal, "I've already tried jumping off a bridge and that didn't work. I tried to overdose on prescriptions and I failed then too. So I guess suicide is only a fantasy. I don't have the courage I had five years ago when I stepped off that bridge. My boldness has turned to timidity." I detested myself for my cowardice and my inability to act.

Early one Sunday afternoon, the Wazeters received a phone call from Nora Lee, an across-the-street neighbor, and one of Mary's closest friends. Nora reported she'd just talked to Mary and that Mary had sounded terribly depressed and had talked about suicide. Mary's parents immediately called Judy and her husband, Bill, in Virginia and urged them to investigate. But when Judy and Bill rushed to Mary's apartment they found, to everyone's relief, that Mary's mood had changed. She was in fact busy preparing quiche for the expected visit of a friend.

A short while after Bill and Judy returned to their home, however, Mary got a call saying her friend couldn't make it after all. And her mood plunged again to the point that hopelessness finally overcame her fear. With her roommate Nan still gone for a few more hours, Mary decided the time had come. But her quick search of the apartment turned up only one prescription bottle of medication—a powerful antidepressant called Amitriptyline. Hoping it was enough to finish the job, Mary downed the nearly full bottle of pills and lay down on her bed to die.

Chapter 27

When Nan came home that same evening to find Mary stretched out on her bed, she assumed Mary was deeply asleep. And when the Wazeters called a little later to talk to their daughter, Nan suggested they call back later in the evening after Mary woke up. However, no sooner had they hung up the phone than Edith Wazeter was struck by a strong sense of troubled concern. Thinking of Nora's earlier call, she mentioned her concern to Leon. He picked up the phone again and redialed the number. Quickly he apprised Nan of their suspicions of another suicide attempt, and urged Nan to again try to rouse Mary. Mary was unresponsive. Nan immediately phoned the Crisis Intervention Unit.

The ambulance arrived within minutes to rush her to the nearest emergency room where doctors pumped her stomach. But she remained in a coma through the night and into the next day. Mary didn't know it, but an overdose of Amitriptyline affects the heart itself and is one drug for which there is no effective known antidote.

How much did Mary take? Enough to kill her? Or just enough to do irreversible heart damage? Doctors could only watch and wait, monitoring her heart through the night. At one point, they say, Mary's heart slowed so dramatically that she was one heartbeat away from death. Even after her pulse began to improve, doctors were fearful of permanent organ damage. When she finally regained consciousness twenty-four hours later, the doctors told her father they'd need a week of observation and testing to assess any lasting damage.

I wish I could tell you that I awakened with a new sense of peace, an unwavering gratitude for another change in life, and an unflinching determination that has carried easily through every hurdle I've faced since that day. But I can't.

I did wake up with much the same heartening "I've-been-given-another-chance feeling" I'd experienced when I regained consciousness after my first overdose. But that positive feeling lasted less than a week.

I wish I could tell you that I checked out of that hospital, turned my life around, and am now living successfully on my own. But I can't say that either.

I did check out a week later with no permanent heart damage. But Judy, who was by then pregnant with her second child, no longer felt she could be responsible for overseeing my care. So my family canceled the Virginia experiment and I returned to my parents' home in Wilkes-Barre at Christmas time, feeling once again like a failure.

I wish I could point to some dramatic turning point, some once-and-for-all decision made at a crisis crossroad, or perhaps some spiritual mountaintop encounter that has transformed my life since I woke up in that hospital. That might make a dramatic and inspirational conclusion to this book. But that hasn't happened.

I wish I could at least say with confident assurance that I've finally reached the point where I know, without a doubt, that I'll never again give in to anorexic or bulimic behavior. But I'm afraid I can't even be certain of that.

And yet I can say this: I'm a very different person from that girl who woke up to find she'd botched yet another suicide attempt. I've found hope and peace again.

The change, though definite, has been gradual. And it's come in a number of small steps taken, small lessons learned.

It may have started shortly after I got out of the hospital when I was riding in the car with Judy, her husband, Bill, and their two-year-old son, David. My little nephew looked at me and, in the sweetest, most gentle voice, he said, "I wuv you, Mary." Those soft-spoken words cut through my despair. And when he said them again, "I wuv you, Mary," it was as if God was speaking to me in the voice of a little child.

Bill felt it too. He said, "That's the voice of the Lord, Mary! He wants you to know he still loves you. Listen to him, Mary."

I was listening and what I heard was a new assurance. That after all my struggles, all my failures, I was still worth something to other people and to God. That no matter what I'd put my family through, no matter how cruel and thoughtless I'd been, no matter how discouraged and hopeless things looked, my family loved me and refused to give up on me. That despite the incredible mess I'd made of my life, despite the number of times I'd fallen or turned away from him, God wanted to forgive me. And he still loved me.

I learned a lot of other little lessons in the weeks and months that followed. I enrolled again at King's College, where I took an Abnormal Psych course that enabled me to identify and define a number of my own experiences. The insights I gained during that course made me feel less like some alien creature and more like a redeemable human being.

As time has passed, I've also gained a more realistic picture of what it means to suffer from eating disorders. More and more researchers are now comparing anorexic/bulimics to alcoholics. Like "recovering alcoholics," who realize they will never be "recovered alcoholics," anorexic/bulimics may need to accept the fact that their tendency toward eating disorders may be with them all their lives—one significant difference being that the human body can learn to exist quite well without alcohol, but not at all without food.

Soon after returning to Wilkes-Barre this last time, I began seeing a Philadelphia psychiatrist, Dr. Harry Doyle, who pretty much limits his practice to hardcore cases with long-standing psychiatric problems. From the very beginning of our time together, he has forced my focus off the past and the whys of what happened, and emphasized the future.

I've once again embraced the goal of independence from my parents—physically, emotionally, and financially. But the prospect no longer panics me because I'm learning to take things one small-concrete-achievable step at a time. Even as I write this, I'm finishing my junior year at King's with a major in psychology and a minor in theology. I recently completed the world-renowned literacy expert Frank Lauback's training course, "Volunteers for Literacy," and I'm now tutoring my first pupil. I've become active in a local church again where I'm finding great fulfillment teaching Sunday school for primary-age children.

I've also begun participating in the Regys FES (Functional Electrical Stimulation) program at a nearby rehab center in Scranton. This exciting new computerized process is geared to spinal cord patients—with the aim of reconditioning and energizing paralyzed leg muscles.

At Dr. Doyle's suggestion, I've now obtained my driver's permit and have started taking driving lessons. Yet another small step in my journey toward independence.

So I'm getting there—one step at a time. Not sprinting all out like I used to do, but pacing myself, moving steadily forward.

I'm also learning the important principle of balance. I understand now how easy it is to lose the delicate balance in life and am constantly working toward blending my physical, emotional, intellectual, social, and spiritual identities.

And I've learned some very important lessons about self-acceptance and expectations—expectations others hold up for me and those I impose on myself. I now know that true self-acceptance, true contentment can never be attained by striving for perfection. Contentment didn't come from achieving a "straight-

A" status as a student, or becoming a champion athlete, or having an attractive figure. Nor will contentment in the future be derived from becoming a champion wheelchair racer, finishing my college degree, finding a challenging job, or even completing a book about my struggles. Satisfaction doesn't come from what we *do;* it is a natural outgrowth of what we *are.*

For me, this lesson is summed up beautifully in the lyrics of Amy Grant's song, "All I Ever Have to Be":

> When the weight of all my dreams
> Is resting heavy on my head
> And the thoughtful words of health and hope
> Have all been nicely said,
>
> But I'm still hurting, wondering
> if I'll ever be the one I think I am—
>
> Then you gently re-remind me
> That you made me from the first
> And the more I try to be the best
> The more I get the worst.
>
> And I realize the good in me is only
> There because of who you are—
> And all I ever have to be
> Is what you made me.
> Any more or less would be
> A step out of your plan.
>
> As you daily recreate me
> Help me always keep in mind
> That I only have to do what I can find.
>
> And all I ever have to be . . .
> All I ever have to be
> Is what you made me.*

I'm learning to find this kind of self-acceptance in my personal relationship with God. As I experience his forgiveness and acceptance, I learn to forgive and accept myself—with all my continuing problems and faults.

I can't say, as I wanted to say in the "first conclusion" of this book two years and two chapters ago: "God has healed me and I can walk again." I can't even say, as I planned to say then, that "God has healed me of my anorexia and bulimia."

What I can say, what I want to say is this: "God is healing me now. And he's not nearly done yet."

I may even fall again. But I'm hopeful that the lessons I've already learned will enable me to scramble back up more quickly in the future. I still can't see the finish line. But that's okay, because I know now that real spiritual and emotional healing and growth is a lifelong, marathon process. And with God's help I intend to stay in this race to the very end.

Mary Wazeter began her running career at the age of twelve. It ended at nineteen just as she reached the brink of athletic stardom. Her disturbing and inspiring story has appeared in *Young Miss, Campus Life, People* magazine, *Seventeen* magazine and the *New York Times.* Mary has also related her experience on NBC's *Today Show* and ABC's *World News Tonight.*

Gregg Lewis is an editor and freelance author who has written over three hundred magazine articles and ten books, including *The Hurting Parent, Beyond a Broken Promise,* and *In Sickness and in Health.*